A
PASTORAL
COUNSELING
CASEBOOK

BY

C. Knight Aldrich, M. D.
and
Carl Nighswonger, B. D., S. T. M.

THE WESTMINSTER PRESS
Philadelphia

LIBRARY OF CONGRESS CATALOG CARD No. 68-24677

Published by The Westminster Press ®
Philadelphia, Pennsylvania

PRINTED IN THE UNITED STATES OF AMERICA

ACKNOWLEDGMENTS

The authors acknowledge with gratitude the contributions, reported in this book, of the participants in the seminars organized by the Chaplain's Office of the University of Chicago Clinics. Not only did they supply the case material, but their willingness to speak freely about their feelings and frustrations, and their constructive challenges to the conventional stereotypes of counseling provided the spark that made the seminars exciting and that convinced us that they were worth reporting.

We also acknowledge with appreciation the generous contribution of the Butz Foundation toward the preparation of the manuscript for publication, and the painstaking and imaginative editorial contribution of Carol Aldrich in translating a tape-recorded transcription into a readable manuscript.

CONTENTS

INTRODUCTION

The purpose of this book is to help clergymen feel more confident in counseling parishioners who come to them with emotional problems. These parishioners make up a substantial part of the mental health problem in the United States. According to a national study conducted for the Joint Commission on Mental Illness and Health, 42 percent of people who seek help for emotional or psychological problems go first to the clergy.

This proportion may seem somewhat surprising in view of the traditional role of the family physician as the first source of help for emotional problems. But as patterns of medical care continue to change in the direction of increasing specialization, the family doctor is not as available as he used to be. Psychiatrists and other mental health professionals are in short supply and are concentrated in urban areas. They cannot take the family physician's place in the front line of mental health care even if there were no psychological obstacles to their doing so.

Unlike psychiatrists, the parish clergy are well represented geographically, and are available to persons irrespective of class or socio-economic and educational levels. There are indeed many counties and sections of the country where the clergy are the only resources to whom individuals can appeal for help with problems. Although there are some barriers to ready accessibility to the clergy, such as the image of the church as the "community of the elect," or the anticipation that a clergyman may be moral-

9

istic, judgmental, or punitive, there seems to be less psychological distance between layman and clergyman than between layman and psychiatrist or other professional mental health resources. (Richard V. McCann, *The Churches and Mental Health*, p. 233; Basic Books, 1962.)

People whose emotional symptoms resemble medical conditions tend to seek help primarily from medical sources. The problems that are taken to the clergy are more likely to be presented in psychological or interpersonal terms. Two thirds of the problems brought to pastoral counselors concern marital and family difficulties and "psychological distress." Next in order of frequency are adolescent behavior problems, problems of illness and aging, and problems caused by alcoholism. Religious and spiritual questions come only sixth in frequency. (*Ibid.*, p. 79.)

In view of this preponderance of psychological problems in the counseling ministry, it is not surprising that clergymen are beginning to look more to psychological than to theological sources for assistance in their efforts to help their parishioners. The psychiatrist, medically trained in the care of emotional disorders, is a logical source of professional guidance for the pastoral counselor. However, until recently the relationship between psychiatrists and clergymen has been neither easy nor productive. Many of the participants in the seminars from which this book is adapted had felt disappointed and frustrated in their previous contacts with psychiatrists.

Much of the difficulty seemed to arise from differences between the two professions, both in underlying assumptions and in *modus operandi*. For example, since the clergyman's role includes the obligation to provide whatever help he can to anyone who comes to him, he is often puzzled and angry when a psychiatrist does not accept one of his parishioners as a patient. Communication about referrals is another potential source of frustration. When the psychiatrist does not communicate with the clergyman who has made the referral, he gives an impression of indifference to the minister's concern for his parishioner. Furthermore, the clergyman may find it difficult to understand the psychiatrist's reluctance to share professional and confidential information, especially since in most cases he has already shared his own information.

Still another barrier to a productive relationship between psychiatrists and ministers is the widespread belief among clergymen that all psychiatrists are "godless" enemies of religion. It is true that some of them still feel, as Freud did to some extent, that religion can be harmful to creative human growth and development. Most modern psychiatrists, however, respect their patients' religious ideas whether or not they are congruent with their own personal beliefs and they recognize the therapeutic qualities of a healthy religious attitude as well as the possible pathological uses of religion.

Some parishioners may lose their religious zeal during psychotherapy, or perhaps may even have their faith undermined. Much depends on the nature of the relationship between their faith and their emotional disorders. A person who is emotionally disturbed or troubled may bring his religious beliefs and concerns into his distorted framework of pathological behavior, attempting to "use" his religion in his illness. Certainly, any clergyman familiar with the patient population of a state mental hospital has encountered many actively "religious" persons who have incorporated religious concerns into their delusional behavior patterns.

Perhaps a more common illustration is the parishioner whose neurotic needs for self-punishment have found an ally in the religious teachings of his church, so that the moral demands of a responsible religious concern have been reinterpreted in a self-destructive manner. The late Paul Tillich emphasized the dangers of "quasi religion," which serves as a defense against life by helping the individual conceal, manipulate, or distort reality. This use of religious ideas may well prevent the individual from developing a more mature religious faith. In such cases, the loss of quasi religion in treatment may be a necessary preliminary step toward religious as well as emotional maturity.

In spite of the barriers to effective communication between the professions, modern clergymen have begun to ask for more information and guidance from psychiatrists, particularly in their efforts to diagnose the parishioner's problem. But, although theological education has begun to recognize the importance of helping the clergyman develop diagnostic skills in his counseling ministry, this training still represents only a small fraction of the clergyman's education. Theological training often has emphasized treatment procedures, on the assumption that all men can be adequately diagnosed as sinners in need of repentance. This oversimplified assessment fails to help the minister recognize the manifestations of specific psychological problems in concrete counseling situations. However, if the clergyman develops an effective method of organizing the information he receives so that he can accurately assess his parishioners' problems, he will then be able to plan his interventions in treatment to fit the specific case; he will have more confidence in his use of interventions and will therefore be less likely to rely on a general formula for counseling.

Although more emphasis on diagnosis would be desirable, theological training cannot and should not make the clergyman a fully trained therapist. It is almost inevitable, therefore, that when he undertakes his parish ministry, he will face problems that he is not equipped to manage and he may want to consult with a psychiatrist.

Psychiatric consultation is not always easy for the pastor to find. Psychiatrists have only recently begun to recognize the importance of providing consultation for community caregivers. Some are still doubtful, believing that the amount of training that can practically be provided for clergymen will not give enough protection to the parishioner. They recommend restriction of the pastoral counseling function to superficial supportive assistance with a heavy reliance on referral. We believe, on the other hand, that some risks will have to be taken if pastoral counseling is to make its optimum contribution to the mental health of the nation.

> There is always present the risk that the relief obtained through pastoral counseling may cover over and otherwise disguise deep-lying emotional conflicts and personality needs. This risk can be reduced by providing the clergy with information and understanding, preferably through training and some variety of clinical experience, so that they can more readily recognize symptoms of pathology and also so that they can have enough insight to see clearly the limits of their own competence. In the long run the risk seems worth taking, particularly when it is weighed against the woefully inadequate professional manpower and facilities available for treatment. (*Ibid.*, p. 238.)

As psychiatrists become more active in the community, consultation should be easier for the clergyman to find. Some clergymen will establish individual contacts with psychiatrists, while others set up groups of pastors to meet with a consultant at regular intervals. This sharing of problems and insights may prove the most efficient use of the psychiatrist's and of the minister's time.

The successful application of such interdisciplinary cooperation requires the pastor's understanding of his own professional roles and purposes. He must be aware of the multiple dimensions of his pastoral relationships with parishioners. He cannot structure his pastoral relationships in the same way that the psychiatrist structures his therapeutic relationships. Most psychiatrists can remain aloof from their patients outside the office; the clergyman continues to carry out his ministerial responsibilities with the parishioners whom he counsels. The multiple nature of the pastor-parishioner relationship thus provides the minister with a much broader context in which to work than that of the psychiatrist. The clergyman who overidentifies with the psychiatric model will fail to take advantage of the multiplicity of his pastoral contacts.

The professional isolation in which many parish clergymen

must work makes it difficult for them to recognize or deal with their own feelings, especially with respect to the "problem" parishioner. The clergyman's unrecognized feelings toward a particular person may not only adversely affect his counseling ministry, but may negatively influence other dimensions of his pastoral relationships to that person as well as to his family. Consultation with a psychiatrist may help the pastor see that his own feelings can interfere with his role as counselor and with the quality of counseling he is providing. It can also help him find a realistic balance between his own need to help his parishioners and the actual needs of those who come to him for counseling.

The original impetus for writing this book came from the Chaplain's Office of the University of Chicago Clinics, which has for some time been concerned with the continuing education of clergy in the local community. Programs started by Rev. Granger Westberg in Religion and Medicine have been continued first by the late Rev. Carl Wennerstrom and now by Rev. Carl Nighswonger. When participants in these programs expressed an interest in more intensive and specific assistance in pastoral counseling, Chaplain Nighswonger organized a seminar-workshop which ran for five half days in the winter of 1965, inviting Dr. C. Knight Aldrich to lead it.

The group was composed of twenty clergymen from the greater Chicago area. They were approximately evenly divided between inner-city and suburban congregations in a wide variety of community settings and represented a number of established churches, primarily, though not exclusively, Protestant. The small size of the group ensured the maximum participation and interchange of ideas. For the first meeting, each participant was asked to submit in writing a summary of a problem case in his counseling ministry. From these summaries, Dr. Aldrich and Chaplain Nighswonger selected those which seemed most representative of the types of cases commonly encountered by the clergy. After an introductory session on personality development, these cases formed the basis of the seminars.

The discussions were recorded on tape and transcribed, and the transcripts were then edited with two goals in mind: to adapt the free and informal style of the discussions to a more organized and coherent written form, and at the same time to preserve the flavor and spontaneity of the original sessions. Throughout the manuscript, great care has been taken to maintain confidentiality by disguising the details of the case histories and by giving fictitious names to the subjects. In each chapter, the pastor presenting the case has been identified by a fictitious name and the other participants by numbers.

In summary, the growing recognition of the parish clergyman as a "firing-line professional" to whom almost half of all troubled people turn first for help has pointed out the unique and extremely significant position of the counseling ministry. The responsible fulfillment of this role requires of the clergyman not only a clear understanding of his pastoral identity, but an awareness of the potential resources available to him from psychiatry and from other disciplines concerned with the welfare of troubled persons. We hope that this book will provide a model of one kind of consultative relationship and that it will encourage the clergyman to explore consultative relationships in his own community.

Chapter One

INTRODUCTION
TO
PERSONALITY DEVELOPMENT

The understanding of a specific person is easier to work out if it is based on a general framework of personality structure and development. Such a framework provides a means of organizing one's thinking about a patient or a client or a parishioner whom one is trying to help. The case discussions, therefore, are prefaced with a descriptive chapter by Dr. Aldrich. This provides a schematic outline of the psychological development and function of the normal, or average, personality.

The framework I have found most useful is in two dimensions. One dimension is developmental—a historical dimension on a time axis. It is represented in the form of a ladder in Figure 1. The other dimension is structural, and is represented symbolically in the circle diagram (Figure 2). In this diagram the personality is pictured as a circle surrounded by and interacting with the environment. The environment includes both personal and nonpersonal elements, but the environmental stresses that interfere with the free expression of inner drives and impulses, and are therefore of greatest significance to the understanding of personality, are personal. This emphasis doesn't mean that cold and hunger, or the necessity to adapt to cold and hunger, are ignored, but it does mean that in our society the problems that stir up emotional conflict are usually related to other people.

17

Fig. I PERSONALITY DEVELOPMENT

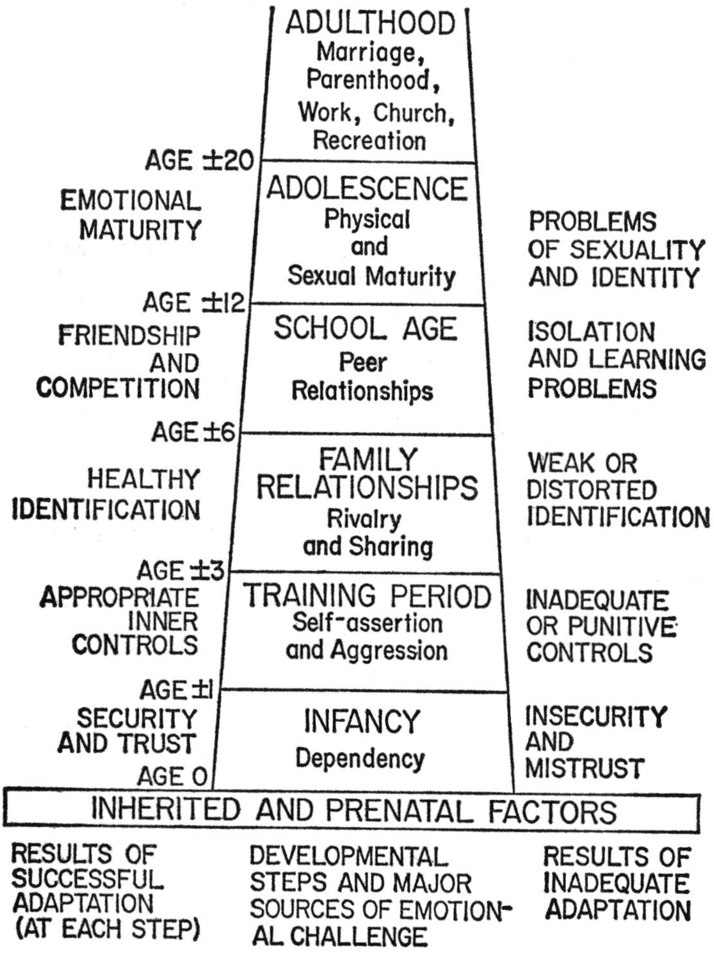

RESULTS OF SUCCESSFUL ADAPTATION (AT EACH STEP)	DEVELOPMENTAL STEPS AND MAJOR SOURCES OF EMOTIONAL CHALLENGE	RESULTS OF INADEQUATE ADAPTATION
	ADULTHOOD Marriage, Parenthood, Work, Church, Recreation	
AGE ±20		
EMOTIONAL MATURITY	**ADOLESCENCE** Physical and Sexual Maturity	PROBLEMS OF SEXUALITY AND IDENTITY
AGE ±12		
FRIENDSHIP AND COMPETITION	**SCHOOL AGE** Peer Relationships	ISOLATION AND LEARNING PROBLEMS
AGE ±6		
HEALTHY IDENTIFICATION	**FAMILY RELATIONSHIPS** Rivalry and Sharing	WEAK OR DISTORTED IDENTIFICATION
AGE ±3		
APPROPRIATE INNER CONTROLS	**TRAINING PERIOD** Self-assertion and Aggression	INADEQUATE OR PUNITIVE CONTROLS
AGE ±1		
SECURITY AND TRUST	**INFANCY** Dependency	INSECURITY AND MISTRUST
AGE 0		
	INHERITED AND PRENATAL FACTORS	

Fig. 2 PERSONALITY STRUCTURE

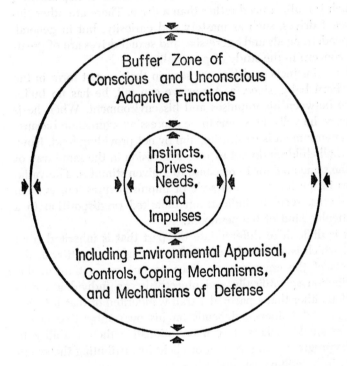

ENVIRONMENTAL STRESSES AND CHALLENGES

Buffer Zone of
Conscious and Unconscious
Adaptive Functions

Instincts,
Drives,
Needs,
and
Impulses

Including Environmental Appraisal,
Controls, Coping Mechanisms,
and Mechanisms of Defense

INSTINCTS AND DRIVES

No one yet knows the exact nature of the drives and impulses, and no one knows how much they are determined by heredity and how much by environment. Fortunately, the practical application of psychiatry need not be based on a detailed theory of instincts. For practical purposes it is enough to recognize that three drives or needs are primarily responsible for people's conflicts with their environment, with one another, and with themselves. First is the aggressive drive, expressed either as a demand for something that the environment withholds, or as an impulse to get rid of something that is irritating or frustrating. Second is the sexual drive and third is dependency, which is really a need rather than a drive. There are other significant drives, such as mastery and curiosity, but in general, dependent needs and aggressive and sexual drives are of greatest concern in the study of personality.

Basic instincts or drives are seen in their purest form in the newborn baby, since, as far as we can tell, he has no buffer zone between his impulses and his environment. When he is hungry, he yells; he seems to be expressing aggression because his environment is frustrating him by not providing food. However, all children do not express aggression in the same way or in the same amount in response to a given stimulus. The variations in the intensity and style of impulse expression, even in newborns, seem to indicate an inherited predisposition to a particular kind of temperament.

It is difficult to differentiate the part that is inherited from that which is acquired early in life through maturation or the effects of the environment. Since no one can yet make this distinction scientifically and objectively, an individual's conviction either that a particular trait is inherited or that it is due to parental influence depends on his own subjective needs. Professional workers, too, may rationalize their inability to make progress with a patient or client by attributing the symptoms to hereditary causes.

INFANCY

The relationship of the newborn child to his environment is primarily dependent, since he is unable to do anything for himself. The helpless and dependent infant seems to develop his concept of the world in terms of the response to his needs by those around him. If he is not cared for, or if he must wait for adult convenience, he gets the impression that the world is not a very good place. Since he can't communicate directly, no one can be sure how he really feels, but extrapolation back from later experience justifies this assumption. People who have not developed a sense of security generally have experienced an unsatisfactory response to their early dependent needs. On the other hand, a sense of security and of trust in others usually does develop in the infant who is taken care of and whose needs are responded to when he is helpless.

Some parents are afraid that immediate response to their child's dependent needs will spoil him. I don't believe, however, that a child will be spoiled if his parents respond to needs he is unable to satisfy on his own. There is an important difference between responding to needs he cannot satisfy and responding to needs he can. If an eight-year-old child says, "Mother, go upstairs and get the books I left on the table," and she goes up and gets them, she is in a sense spoiling him because he is perfectly capable of doing it himself. A mother's intervention to feed her helpless infant when he is hungry does not have the same implications. In fact, if she doesn't feed him, he is entitled to feel anxious and frustrated, and perhaps angry.

Modern understanding of personality is based on the belief that when the dependent needs that an infant cannot satisfy by himself are satisfied by others, he tends to develop a sense of security, a feeling of belongingness, and a concept of the world as a place where he can count on others when he is in trouble. There is some evidence that after four months of age, when he can distinguish between individuals, the child not only requires satisfaction of his dependent needs, but requires a single person (usually, though not necessarily, the mother) to provide this security. At about four months he begins to sense who is his usual supplier of needs; if for some reason he loses the support of this person, he may not only mistrust her but may extend this feeling to include other people as well. Mistrust then may become a part of his personality structure so that he either continues indefinitely to seek assurance that he will be cared for, or avoids dependency as much as possible because his early experience has been so frightening. These characteristics remain part of his personality all his life, although they are particularly evident when he is sick or under stress.

TRAINING PERIOD

For the first year or so the child remains reasonably helpless and dependent. Then he begins to learn to walk and talk, and to learn how to manipulate things. He begins to assert himself and to make his wants known in a more active way. Up to this point, those around him have been able either to meet or not to meet his needs as suited their convenience; but now he can be more insistent, and his parents start setting limits to his demands. His self-assertion and his aggressive impulses begin to run into barriers to their expression. In the next two years or so, he struggles with his parents for a chance to assert and express himself, and they struggle to channel his self-assertion into civilized forms of behavior. Eventually, as his understanding develops, he begins to incorporate some of the parental barriers so that he can avoid constant conflict with the parental environment. He begins to develop mechanisms to cope with the conflict between what he wants and what the world outside wants of him. These coping mechanisms become a kind of buffer zone between his inner needs and impulses and the outer environmental demands.

As the buffer zone develops, the child gradually learns to give up or to delay the immediate satisfaction of his needs and his drives. The child who likes to play with bric-a-brac, and whose mother has told him "No" about eight million times, finally begins to tell himself "No." Before it becomes really part of him so he doesn't have to think about it, he says, "No, mustn't touch," to himself, and then he doesn't touch. After a while it becomes automatic, so that he doesn't have to go through the procedure of telling himself "No"; it takes place below the level of his consciousness, or *unconsciously,* and happens without his even being aware of the stimulus.

As time goes on, a great deal of psychological activity becomes unconscious. Appraisal of the environment, inhibition or delay of response, and substitution of indirect for direct responses can all be unconscious as well as conscious processes.

Although the inhibiting and delaying and substituting functions are gradually developing throughout the one- to three-year-old period, they usually aren't too effective until some time between two and a half and three. Meanwhile, self-assertion develops in a crescendo until, by the time the child is about two and a half, the parents have reached the end of their patience and think that their little animal is never going to be civilized. At this time, fortunately, a relatively rapid progress of civilization begins, and by the time he is three, the average child has incorporated family prohibitions in most areas. Sometimes, however, he reserves one area in which to continue the struggle with the parents, usually an area that the parents unconsciously select. Although the parents are seldom aware that they have selected a battlefield, they provide the child with signals that indicate where they are vulnerable, and so indirectly encourage him to continue the fight in the area of their vulnerability.

A favorite area for a continuing fight is eating. "I don't want to eat. I won't eat," says little Johnny, recognizing his mother's signal that she is particularly sensitive to the reflection on her ability as a mother which is produced by his refusal to eat. "You've got to eat," says Mother. "I won't," says Johnny. Self-assertion is his major goal at this point in his development, and winning the fight is even more important to him than satisfying his hunger. He can usually outlast his mother, and if he is forced to eat, he often throws the food back in one way or another.

Another combat site is toilet training. Mother says, "You have to do it my way," and Johnny says, "I won't," perhaps not in so many words but in ways that convey this message. A third battleground is intellectual accomplishment. Especially in an intellectual milieu, parents compete through their children's intelligence. In families that regard talking as an important measure of intellectual competence, some children assert themselves by *not* talking. However, if the demand for compliance is not pushed too hard, the child usually begins to talk or eat, or is toilet trained, for his own comfort and sense of maturity, and he finds ways of asserting himself that are not so self-defeating.

When parental controls are generally too permissive, or else too punitive and rigid, the child is likely to develop a general problem with controls, rather than a problem in a specific area. If he does not develop sufficient controls, he may become an impulsive, aggressive personality who always has to have what he wants immediately. If he develops too many controls, he may become an overinhibited person who can't permit himself any self-assertion at all.

There is no certain way of determining which person will become inhibited and which overaggressive. Sometimes in the same family, one child is overaggressive and seems never to have internalized any controls, whereas another child is too scared of the consequences to be aggressive at all. On the other hand, two opposite responses to impulse can be associated in the same person; someone who is impulsive in one way may be overcontrolled in other areas, as he responds to the different parental signals and expectations in different areas.

The Conscience

The incorporated parental and other environmental controls roughly correspond to the conscience. If a child fails to incorporate the standards set up by his family, church, and community, or if his models are corrupt, he may develop no conscience. On the other hand, he may develop an overly harsh and punitive conscience; it is as though, in order to prevent the unacceptable impulse from breaking through, he must frighten himself with the threat of terrible consequences for *any* transgression. The child who develops such a conscience seems unable to differentiate realistically between serious and trivial wrongdoing; any relaxation threatens to break down the barriers that he has set up to protect himself. His standards remain outside himself, an external threat similar to the conception of God as a vengeful authority whose watchful eye cannot be eluded.

According to personality theory, therefore, the conscience is acquired, not innate. There may be innate problems that make it difficult to acquire an adequate conscience, but there is no scientific evidence that the nature of the conscience is determined before birth or early in infancy.

FAMILY RELATIONSHIPS

At the beginning of his development of relationships with other people, the newborn baby is almost exclusively concerned with himself. He acts as if he thought, "I am the center of the universe. Other people are here to take care of me and to let me have what I want." The idea of sharing or giving to others is quite foreign to him. If he has a new brother or sister before he is about three, he cannot enjoy sharing his possessions or his place in the sun, although he may make an effort to do so in the interest of avoiding parental reprisals. Starting at about three, the child begins to be able to relate in a give-and-take way with others, particularly with his parents, and in the next two or three years he tests out his capacity for interpersonal relationships in the family circle.

Meanwhile, he is beginning to comprehend the concept of growth. Most of us underestimate children's understanding of concrete concepts, and overestimate their capacity for abstract thinking. Time is an abstract concept, and the child must be able to conceptualize time in order to conceptualize growth. He responds when Grandma says, "My, how you've grown" or "You're going to be a big man like Daddy," because a response is expected, not because he understands what she means. The child doesn't really understand time and growth until he is close to five or six; at this point he begins to get the idea that childhood is a temporary condition and he can project himself into the future as an adult.

Along with the new idea comes clarification of the difference between male and female social roles. As his understanding of growth and social role develops, the child begins to *identify* with the parent of his own sex. The boy thinks, "I am going to be a grown-up and I'm going to be a man like Daddy," and the girl says to herself, "I'm going to grow up to be a woman like Mommy." But since the boy and the girl are simultaneously struggling to assert themselves, their projections into the future inevitably are associated with rivalry with the parents they expect to emulate. "Whatever Daddy has, I want," says the boy: his car, his fishing gear, and so on. Sitting behind the steering wheel is not taken seriously by the parents at this time but taking father's place with mother presents more of a problem. The child really does have the major part of mother's attention during the day, and then must give up some of it when father returns in the evening and expects his share. Any self-respecting child resents being shoved out of the center of mother's attention and will compete with father for her attention. The boy, perceiving himself as an eventual man, is more likely to emphasize the competition with father, while the girl emphasizes the competition with mother.

The child's rivalry is not only with his parents but with his brothers and sisters. The parental rivalry seems more important, however, because the pattern of adult interpersonal relationships and the choice of marital partners are determined, to a considerable extent, by the patterns the child perceives in his parents. The adult patterns include sexual components, which also seem to be related to the childhood experience of rivalry. Thus, the fact that some men choose wives who resemble their mothers and others choose opposites seems to depend on the kind of relationship the man had with his own mother. A boy who loves his mother but observes that the tie between mother and father is firm can give up the rivalry with his father for first place in his mother's affections, as if he had decided that there was no point in fighting a lost cause. He makes peace with father and in a way strengthens his identification with him, saying, "When I get married, I want someone *like* Mother" —a girl "just like the girl that married dear old Dad."

The man who chooses a girl who is the opposite of his mother may not have abandoned the rivalry with father and so may still be keeping mother in first place in his affections. On the other hand, he may have found mother so unsatisfactory a person that he cannot love anyone who resembles her. It is hard to know which reason explains his choice unless his background and his development are understood; but if he has a marital problem, proper help depends on knowing the reason.

SCHOOL AGE

In the period from about six to about twelve, the school-age period, the child's emotional ties are usually broadened to include friends as well as family. Although in earlier years the child has friends, he is primarily concerned with his family, and the friendships are tenuous. If he still is overly attached to his family, or if he is still preoccupied with family rivalry, it will be hard for him to develop friends outside the family circle.

Each phase of development depends on the previous phases: the child must be reasonably secure before he can concentrate his attention on mastery of his aggressive impulses, he must have harnessed his aggression before he can work out his family relationships, and so on. If the child becomes sufficiently free from preoccupation with his family and has sufficient security and trust so that he doesn't have to keep looking back over his shoulder to find out if mother really is there, he can invest wholeheartedly in his friends. If he is confident in his ability to control aggression, he can compete comfortably in academic, athletic, and social areas. If he is afraid that his aggression will make him hurt somebody, however, he will hold back in the competition and if he lacks control of his impulses, competition will too readily degenerate into a fight.

ADOLESCENCE

Ordinarily the school age is a relaxed period, but the next step, adolescence, is usually more stormy. The biological changes of puberty supercharge the child's affectionate relationships with sexuality and stir up much of the adolescent storm. The eleven-year-old boy who plays comfortably and naturally with little Susie as well as with Joe becomes ill at ease with Sue after he reaches adolescence. The new sexual component of his affectionate relationships frightens him. He is also frightened because he doesn't spontaneously differentiate relationships in which the culture permits love but not sex from those which can combine the two. Eventually most adolescents distinguish between people whom they should only love, like mothers, and people for whom they can feel both love and sexual interest, like girl friends.

Failure to accomplish this division, usually arising from failure to work out family relationships satisfactorily, predisposes the adolescent to conflict in his future heterosexual relationships. Conflict about heterosexual relationships can be combated in various ways. One way is to avoid *any* interest in sex; another is to avoid any interest in the *opposite* sex. A third way is to divide adults of the opposite sex into two categories, good and bad. A boy's love is then for mothers and for pure women who are kept on a pedestal; sex is for impure women whom one can't really respect. In some marriages in which the husband is still attached to his mother, he puts his wife, as a sexual person, in a depreciated position. He may have anticipated this type of relationship by marrying someone whom he considers inferior, rationalizing it as an act of rescue but really making sure that mother remains in first place in his affections.

The adolescent is physically ready to take his place among men before he is an adult educationally and culturally. This discrepancy causes problems with his parents, as he claims, "I am now a man [or a woman] and I have a right to be treated as an adult." He does not want to be taken too seriously, however, because he is still unsure of himself. In some ways he needs limits about which he can feel free to complain without fearing that they will completely give way. He needs a defined but expanding area of experimentation in which he can gain some success, as he overcomes his fear of the adult role. Every time he is successful, his confidence in himself is strengthened; as he learns adult ways of coping, he has progressively less temptation to fall back into a dependent or more childlike role.

ADULTHOOD

The adult recapitulates much of his childhood experience, sometimes directly and sometimes indirectly. In marriage, both in selecting a mate and in maintaining the intimacy of married life, he models his reaction on his family and on other earlier relationships. In parenthood, he vicariously recapitulates the developmental phases with his children. This vicarious participation may interfere with the child's development; for example, a parent may insist that his child receive more education than he did, whether the child wants it or not.

The hierarchical structure of business makes most wage earners dependent on supervisors or other superiors. Those who find dependency severely threatening cannot stand working for others and have to be their own boss; other people are only comfortable when they can depend on a parentlike boss. Early attitudes toward dependency affect an adult's response to the realistic limitations of productivity caused by menopause, retirement, and aging. Early attitudes toward competition influence an adult's business life as well as his play, for example, on the golf links.

An adult's relationship to his church and to you, the church's representative, is also colored by his earlier relationship to parental authority. For that reason, your parishioners will not always see you as you really are. Some will have an idealized image of you as the strong and benevolent authority figure they wish they had found in earlier situations. On the other hand, some of them will see you as a stricter authoritarian than you happen to be, and they will act as though you threaten them with rejection if they do not acquiesce in your wishes. "Who, me?" you say, as you note their apprehension and their obsequiousness. "You don't have to be scared of me!" But parishioners superimpose on you, by a mechanism called *transference,* patterns that they learned early in life to associate with parental authority and that they now associate with all authorities.

Occasionally the pattern is reversed. A man who had a relaxed, lenient pal as a father may, through transference, see you as a confederate rather than as a spiritual adviser. He may attempt to use this interpretation of authority as a means of avoiding some of the responsibilities you would like him to accept. Anyone's response to a clergyman is influenced not only by the church as it is and by the clergyman as he actually is, but by the way in which his perception of authority was influenced by his relationship with his own parents.

For an adult, sickness recapitulates the dependent role and stirs up feelings about helplessness that the sick man may consider he has outgrown. Some sick people seem to be saying, "Good. At last I have what I have been looking for all my life. Now people will have to take care of me." Others seem to be saying, "I can't let myself be sick because I can't trust anybody to care for me." These people second-guess the doctor, because to follow doctor's orders is to be dependent, and they are scared of dependency. Thus sickness, in a way a return to the helplessness of early infancy, reawakens attitudes that have lain dormant since childhood.

Reawakening earlier attitudes, or *regression*, is a characteristic response to stress situations. When the pressure on one rung of the development ladder is too great, a person may slip down to a lower rung. If he has unfinished business from his early developmental phases, he may get caught in the grip of unsolved problems that other people have been able to cope with. He does not bounce back when the crisis is over but persists in inappropriate or *neurotic* patterns of response.

The basic neurotic pattern, or evidence of the presence of unsolved emotional problems, is *anxiety*. Anxiety is usually a sign of a threatened breakthrough of an unacceptable feeling, wish, or thought. It represents the fear that the feeling will be expressed through an unacceptable act which will either damage someone else or will cause damage or loss to the anxious person.

Normal Grief

The stresses that can precipitate neurotic reactions include normal stresses, such as bereavement, that everyone experiences. When one participant in a relationship dies, a part of the survivor is gone, and the survivor "misses" and grieves for the part of himself that is gone as well as for the one who has died. In the same way a person grieves for the loss of part of the body, such as an eye, or the loss of possessions, as when a home burns down. As clergymen, you are familiar with the symptoms of ordinary grief: preoccupation with thoughts of the person who is gone; weeping, sighing, appetite loss, and other physical signs of depression; and inability to focus attention on anything but the loss and the injury to the survivor's extended self.

Ordinarily, it requires about six months for the survivor to carry out his "grief work," to say farewell, as it were, and to reconcile himself to the loss of immediate ties to the deceased. The extent and duration of grief depend to a considerable extent on the amount of need for the deceased and the kind of dependency on him. Gradually a repair process takes place, almost like the healing of a wound, until the survivor adapts to the loss and can resume life without the person who has died.

If some time elapses between the recognition that death is imminent and the actual death, the bereaved can "prepare" himself through grief in anticipation. He may begin to carry out the process of mourning before the person actually dies. For this reason, a sudden death is often more traumatic and disturbing to the survivor than a relatively slow death. If the period of anticipation lasts long enough, virtually all the grief work can be done while the patient is still alive.

A patient's "miraculous" recovery after his family's grief work is done may have a tragic component, for upon recovering he may find a distance between himself and the people he loves. They have finished mourning him, and he is no longer a part of them. The same kind of process occurred during the war, when men who had been missing in action and presumed dead returned home.

PATHOLOGICAL GRIEF

Grief doesn't always run the same course. The pioneer student of the psychology of grief was a Boston psychiatrist named Erich Lindemann, who studied the effects of the Cocoanut Grove nightclub fire in 1942, in which 491 people were killed. Many of those who were severely burned were treated at Massachusetts General Hospital where Lindemann worked, and he took this opportunity to study the process of grief among the survivors and the relatives of the dead. He pointed out that grief which is not actively expressed is likely to persist for a longer time. If grief is covered, or hidden from view, it remains like an abscess to cause trouble later on. Lindemann concluded, therefore, that it is important to help bereaved people express their feelings of grief soon after their bereavement.

This need has been recognized for centuries; it is the major psychological reason for funeral ceremonies and procedures. Although the ceremonies can be overdone, certainly as far as the cost is concerned, and the emotional need can be exploited, the basic psychological function of a funeral is to help people grieve. The wake, too, provides an opportunity for people to help each other express grief; both wakes and funerals counteract to some extent the opposite cultural pressure to conceal their feelings.

What keeps some people from expressing grief? A major reason is a mixture of positive and negative feelings—*ambivalent* feelings—toward the person who has died. If the survivor feels guilty about the amount of anger he felt toward that person, it is difficult for him to grieve to the point of really saying farewell, because he must say farewell with all his feelings, not just with the positive ones. Angry feelings, insofar as they retain their earliest and most primitive significance, mean, "I'm glad you're dead." The ambivalent survivor acts as if he cannot say, "I'm sorry that you are dead," without at the same time saying, "I am also glad that you are dead," and he feels too guilty about the glad feelings to permit them to emerge into consciousness.

Even when delayed or disguised grief begins to be expressed directly, there is no assurance that it will be worked out at a normal pace, because the same factors that made it difficult to express it at all may produce a prolonged grief reaction. I am sure you are familiar with people in your congregations who at first expressed no grief following a loss, but once the floodgates were opened continued almost indefinitely to express their grief.

The ambivalence that prevents the normal expression of grief may not be directly related to the deceased person. I remember one family whose daughter was killed in an automobile accident. Her father was devastated—he was immobilized, crushed, unable to go to work or even to make the funeral arrangements. His wife, on the other hand, carried on "beautifully," took care of everything, made all the funeral arrangements, kept up the house, and served sandwiches to people who called.

Gradually, during the next six months, the father got over his grief, and began to resume his normal activities. But the first time he went out to play golf, his wife became furious with him, saying bitterly, "How can you go out and enjoy yourself with our daughter dead?" Shortly thereafter she lost her voice, and continued speechless for two years before she finally could be helped. She had no physical illness: the loss of her voice was a physical substitute for her unexpressed grief, a *conversion reaction* (conversion, as psychiatrists use it, is the term for the substitution of a symbolic physical symptom for repressed conflictful emotion). Her grief was, therefore, delayed, concealed, and prolonged.

This woman was not particularly ambivalent about the girl who had died. However, shortly before the accident, the maternal grandmother had been living in the home. She was an old dragon if ever there was one: an interfering, dominating, controlling, talkative old lady whom nobody liked. When the husband finally couldn't stand her any longer, he insisted, over his wife's somewhat token resistance, that they move her to a nursing home. The subsequent death of the daughter was interpreted by the wife as punishment for what she had done to her mother. The ambivalence that contributed to the delay in her grief reaction to her daughter's death was ambivalence about her mother, not about her daughter. To understand her grief, it was necessary to look beyond her relationship with her daughter.

An overwhelming grief reaction does not necessarily imply ambivalence. Overwhelming grief may result from the loss of someone on whom the survivor has been especially dependent. Most of you have in your parishes or congregations an unmarried woman, perhaps in her forties, who is taking care of a mother in her seventies. The daughter's whole life has been centered on taking care of her mother while her brothers and sisters have gone off to get married. What will happen to the daughter when the mother dies? She may be overwhelmed with her grief because she has lost so much of her extended self.

Usually, however, the daughter has not accepted her role without some ambivalence. The other siblings are living their own lives, and she is the one who has jumped at mother's beck and call for all these years, often without much credit. When her mother dies, she may feel that it is too late to begin to live her own life. Her resentment about her lost opportunities, which would not have been lost if her mother had died earlier, interferes with the expression of her grief.

GUILT AND SHAME

There is some ambivalence in all relationships; it causes trouble only when there is too much of it, or when there is too much guilt or shame about it. Some people cannot even look at their negative feelings, much less accept them. A person with this problem will sometimes try too hard to sell you the idea that his feelings are all positive. During your bereavement call, he tells you, "I loved my mother!" You don't doubt it, but he persists, "I *really* loved my mother!" "Yes, I heard you the first time," you think. "*I really loved my mother!*" he insists. Whom is he trying to convince? You believed him the first time, but when he keeps telling you the same thing over and over, you begin to wonder if he is trying to convince himself. Must he keep telling himself that he loved his mother because he is afraid or ashamed of that part of his feelings, however small, which is not altogether loving? The fact that someone keeps talking about what a good person his mother or wife was does not always mean that he is disguising ambivalence. But you are sensitive, I'm sure, to the point at which, in Hamlet's mother's phrase, "the lady doth protest too much."

There are many factors encouraging the disguise of ambivalence, and many possible disguises. The person who has to be overly clean is often disguising ambivalence. It is natural for the housewife to clean the parlor when the minister is coming to call. But what if she has to clean it half a dozen times? Reality says it was clean the first time and if anything was skipped, it certainly was picked up the second time. The dirt that is being scrubbed the third, fourth, fifth, and sixth times isn't in the parlor, but in her mind. She is trying to prove that she is a clean person, not to you but to herself. Beneath the concern about dirt are angry or hostile or sexual feelings about which she feels ashamed and guilty, and which she identifies as dirty in a symbolic sense.

Psychiatrists and clergymen do not always mean exactly the same thing by "guilt." Guilt to me means the feeling resulting from violation of conscience—a person feels guilty if he does or feels or thinks something that is forbidden by his internal set of standards. "Shame," as I perceive it, is closely related, though not identical; it is the feeling resulting from failure to live up to one's ideal of oneself. If someone thinks (or feels as though he thought, even if the process is not conscious) "that was sinful of me," he feels guilty; if he thinks "that was stupid of me," he feels ashamed. Sometimes it is hard to distinguish the feelings, and a person can think himself sinful and stupid about the same event.

Shame can have other causes; many people are ashamed of physical deformities, for example, which make them different from other people. Someone who breaks his leg and can no longer support his family doesn't necessarily feel guilty, for he hasn't violated his conscience; but he has not lived up to his concept of what he should be and do, and he may therefore feel ashamed, even though others say, "You shouldn't feel ashamed; it wasn't your fault."

As I mentioned earlier, guilt about ambivalence can cause severe trouble in bereavement reactions. Early in his life, when a child is trying to master his aggressive feelings, he does not clearly distinguish between the *feeling* of hostility and hostile *action*. As far as we can tell, the hungry infant assumes that it is his wish that makes the bottle come, and the same assumption applies to hostility. In time, most magical thinking is replaced by more realistic understanding, but if parental prohibitions against a particular type of expression are stringent and are applied early in life, magical thinking may continue. If hostile feelings are stringently prohibited by the parents, the child *represses* them—pushes them down below the surface of his consciousness—and so never has the chance to look at them in an adult, realistic light. This sequence of events makes him particularly vulnerable to bereavement. The hostile wish in its most primitive form is a death wish; if, shortly after wishing his father dead, the child represses this wish to the point of never recognizing hostile feelings toward his father, father's death will appear to be a response to his wish. In other words, it is his wish that killed father, and therefore, in a psychological sense, he feels guilty of murder.

Any bereavement produces depressed feelings in the survivor during his period of mourning. However, this combination of circumstances can contribute to the prolongation of grief after the death of someone toward whom the survivor feels even a little ambivalence. If he has been taught to think of any hostility as sinful, interpreting "Honor thy father and thy mother" to mean that one should never have a single angry thought about father and mother, and if he has learned this interpretation at a time when every angry thought seems dangerous and lethal to him, and has hidden his anger from himself ever since, he will feel disproportionately guilty when the person does die.

DEPRESSION

When the anger that is hidden beneath the disproportionate guilt is turned around and directed at oneself, this self-hatred is manifested as depression. A person with a depression of this kind, however, is not aware of his hate, and simply to explain to him that he really hated the deceased relative whom he mourns does not relieve his depression.

The tendency to direct hostility inward builds up over several years. It usually starts, as I have suggested, in the second developmental period if a child learns that to express hostility is totally unacceptable to his parents. This response cannot be overcome simply by insight or the voice of authority. As a matter of fact, if the depressed person is forced to recognize his hostility before he is ready to, it may make him feel even more guilty and turn more anger at himself, or it may make him reject the person who is trying to help him. In that case he says to himself, "This person who thinks he can help me obviously doesn't understand what it is all about," and so all or part of the relationship is lost. For these reasons, the counselor's interpretations ought to be couched in tentative terms and should not be too far from that particular person's range of acceptability.

Although understanding the basis of someone's emotional disturbance does not *ipso facto* mean that he is going to get well, it can help us understand how to manage the problem. For example, it can help us realize that sympathy may not be the best treatment for the man whose depression is due to self-hate. He feels so guilty that he believes he doesn't deserve anybody's sympathy, and the more sympathy he gets, the more guilty he becomes. So psychiatrists ordinarily treat this type of depression with a degree of firmness and expect a little more of him than he thinks he can produce. We attempt to relieve him of the necessity to punish himself, without expressing hostility toward him. Firmness and definite expectation of performance are usually more helpful than sympathy and relief from the expectation of performance.

A second kind of depression is due to shame at failure to live up to one's standards. The standards may or may not be realistic, and a person who is trying to live up to an impossible standard may feel ashamed and depressed even though nobody could live up to it. As in the depression due to self-hate, insight alone—simply pointing out that his standard is unrealistic—does not often help. It is more helpful to ask him first to clarify the significant standard and then to express an interest in understanding just how he arrived at it. Usually it soon becomes evident that the person doesn't expect other people to live up to his impossibly high code and that his standard reflects the unrealistic expectations of a parent. Clarifying the origin of his high standard leads to his own recognition of its unrealistic nature; it is a step toward the substitution of more realistic standards and may help to relieve his depression.

If a person can't live up to his standards, his self-esteem is bound to be low, and to help a person raise his self-esteem requires something that comes close to sympathy; thus, the attitude that can help a depression due to shame may be harmful to a depression due to guilt. However, many—perhaps most—depressions are due to a combination of shame and hostility turned inward. If one attitude is appropriate for one situation and almost an opposite attitude is appropriate for another situation, it is perplexing when both exist in the same person. Since it is hard to be simultaneously firm and sympathetic, the problem is to decide whether guilt or shame is the most significant factor in a particular depression.

In most cases, except when hostility turned inward is so severe that there is an immediate risk of suicide, you don't have to decide about your attitude right away. When in doubt, wait. This doesn't mean that you do absolutely nothing, but if you are in doubt about which of these two opposite attitudes will be helpful, it is better to wait until you figure out just where you are than to go plunging ahead on an assumption that isn't backed up by facts.

A third kind of depression dates back to the first rung of the child's developmental ladder. It stems from a lack of security, a lack of a feeling of belongingness or of being loved, which makes it difficult for the person to give love later on. No one is more lonely than the person who has never felt love, and therefore has never really been able to give love. The loneliness that comes from a lack of the capacity to share or to exchange love is the cause of many long-standing, almost lifelong, depressions.

It might seem reasonable to assume that you would treat a person with this type of depression by making him feel loved and by trying to compensate for what he missed in his earliest years. But although this course at first seems logical, it doesn't work. It is a hopeless task to try to compensate for a lifelong deprivation. No one can give him enough to make it up. Some people of this kind are quite dependent and will absorb and absorb and absorb. The people around them give and give and give to them, but nothing seems to happen; the more they give, the more is demanded, and eventually they have to quit, either because they are drained or because realistically they have to give to others as well. Other people who have not received early love and security may be so distrustful of love from any human being that they must seek external substitutes, such as alcohol.

People who cannot find lasting relief from their loneliness through relationships with individuals may find a satisfying relationship with an institution that offers a diffuse, less intense but nevertheless personalized dependent tie. A hospital may serve this purpose, but a church is potentially an even better source, provided that the compassion of the pastor or of individual members of the church does not encourage the conversion of the institutional tie into an individual relationship. These people often can sustain a relationship with an intangible God whom they cannot see much better than one with a tangible pastor whom they can see.

I have described three kinds of depression. A fourth kind is part of a more severe mental illness or *psychosis,* such as manic-depressive psychosis or schizophrenia. These depressions are usually so severe or are accompanied by such evident distortions of thinking that they are clearly not appropriate for anyone but a psychiatrist to treat. However, many such patients, particularly those who have passed the acute stage, will return to the community, and the clergyman may be the person best situated to give them help in their readjustment.

I do not think that you should carry the responsibility for helping patients discharged from mental hospitals without some kind of psychiatric assistance. If you are trying to help a patient to readjust after being discharged, you are entitled to information that will guide you in your efforts. If you don't get it, I think you should complain vociferously until you do. At the same time, bear in mind that a psychiatrist in a state hospital may have as many as three hundred patients to care for, and he can't remember them all. If you call him up and say, "Doctor, how do I go about managing Mrs. Jones whom you discharged a month ago and who has now turned up on my doorstep saying she wants me to help her?" he may say, "Mrs. Jones? Who is she?" Even if he can track down her record, he may not find enough information to be very helpful. So, in practical terms, it may be impossible to get as much help as you would like. In any case, however, you can ask, "Well, Doctor, from what you do know about her, and from what I have told you about her today, do you think it is reasonably safe for me to continue exploring emotional problems and environmental problems with her?" You *should* put him on the spot. If he says, "No, stay away," you should put him on a second spot by asking: "What am I supposed to do with her? Where should I send her?" If his first answer is simply, "Yes, I think she is stabilized and I think it would be helpful if you saw her," you've done what you could to get support, even though it leaves you without much useful information.

Summary

In this chapter I have skimmed the surface of personality development and personality structure. In introducing the subject of personality disorder, I have concentrated on grief and depression rather than on anxiety, not because these subjects are intrinsically more important, but because they seem to appear more frequently in pastoral counseling. In subsequent chapters, as we discuss case histories selected from pastoral settings, many of the points I have mentioned will come up again. The framework presented here will be amplified in the practical situations.

In discussing these cases I will try to extrapolate from the limited material available to us, in order to generalize about various problem situations and to outline the developments to be anticipated under ordinary circumstances. In any individual case, details would emerge that tended to confirm or to refute our formulations.

Before we proceed to the case material, let me warn you that we are not going to come out with simple answers, or perhaps with any clear-cut answers at all. The cases presented by the participants in this seminar are not easy to treat. The pastor, like the medical practitioner, has to face the fact that he will not be able to help everybody as much as he would like to, and that he must restrict his major investment of time and effort in counseling to problems that he has some hope of modifying. He does not ignore the others, but he does not set his sights too high.

Chapter Two

UNRESOLVED GRIEF

The case of Ann shows how ambivalent feelings can prevent the expression and resolution of grief. The differences between the psychiatrist's and the clergyman's concepts of grief are contrasted with the similarities in their approaches to helping the grieving person. The discussion of Ann's case focuses on how Mr. Armstrong can help his parishioner express grief, and on how, in doing so, he can make a valuable contribution in the area of preventive psychiatry.

MR. ARMSTRONG: Ann is fifty years old, and is married to Arthur, a retired business executive. They have a married daughter who is twenty-four and had a son who was recently killed at nineteen.

Ann is very active in the church. She sings in the choir and she instituted a prayer group, which troubled me because of her convictions about faith healing; she felt that the prayer group was going to solve all the problems of illness in the church. I talked with her about it, and last year while we were working it out the boy was in an automobile accident. He had been drinking, and she had argued with him about it. He drove off in anger, had the accident a few minutes later, and was killed instantly.

Long before this accident, Ann told me that she had felt guilty about this boy all along as he was not Arthur's child.

Arthur had never been adequate sexually, and during the war Ann had had an affair. He knew about the affair and had been very much upset about it; he had told the boy that he was not his father. Arthur is by no means the dominant person in the family, and Ann is very assertive and domineering. He can't seem to find anything satisfying to do and has found it difficult to adjust to retirement, particularly since he had been used to authority.

I have encouraged them to have Arthur make some of the decisions that Ann has almost automatically made, and I have tried to get them to communicate better. It's discouraging, though. They don't talk to each other about their plans, for example, as far as vacations and trips are concerned. Ann said yesterday that Arthur had left the day before—just packed his bag and said he was leaving for his mother's home in the next state. She said: "I put a book, *Prayer Can Change Your Life,* in his suitcase, hoping that he would read it. If he would just pray, our situation would be different." But I think that she sees prayer primarily as a way of manipulating people.

She was always a rebel in her family home, against church as well as family, and she married a man of whom her parents disapproved. She is still rebelling in church. She wants a memorial tablet to her son put in the church, although the rules of the church, as she well knows, do not permit it. She objects to this restriction and is trying to influence the church to make an exception.

I have had a problem in counseling her, resulting from her chain-smoking. The trustees have said that there will be no smoking anywhere in the new annex of the church. She says: "I cannot accept this restriction. It means that they are trying to put me outside the church. They won't accept me as I am." She insists that this is the case in spite of the fact that she can smoke anywhere except in the annex.

She relates her feelings about smoking to her family. She wasn't allowed to smoke in her home until she was twenty-five, and her father did not know she smoked until she was thirty.

She says, "I am psychotic as far as my smoking is concerned." She claims that she is unable to pray with the group because the building does not have the spirit of God within it, as a result of the smoking restriction. She says she does not want them to change the rule for her, but I doubt that.

DR. ALDRICH: I suspect that she tries so hard to separate God and her father in her own mind that when the smoking restriction turned up in God's house, the spirit of God left. Do you think her attitude represents an attempt to be dominant and controlling in the church as well as in the family? Or do you think it could be a rationalization for a feeling of alienation from the church? In order to avoid the pain of alienation, she might be assigning an external reason for the feeling and saying in effect: "It is not my sin or my guilt that makes me feel outside the church. It is the church's unreasonable restriction about smoking that alienates me."

MR. ARMSTRONG: The members of the choir are very sympathetic to her.

DR. ALDRICH: I am sure they are. But perhaps the more they try to make her feel welcome and accepted, the more guilty she feels about her son.

MR. ARMSTRONG: Ann's daughter had problems too. She rebelled against her parents by marrying someone of another faith. Ann did not really understand her as an adolescent and used her to do much of the housework while she herself was busy around the parish. I don't mean she is a busybody; she helps in many real ways. She is sympathetic to people who are ill, and she does a lot of visiting with shut-ins.

Although the family's problems are complicated, my first objective is to help them face the boy's death. The two parents responded differently at the time. Arthur was broken up about it; he still has not quite accepted it, and I think his trip is specifically to see the boy's grave. He feels somehow responsible and also guilty because he had made such an issue of the fact that this boy wasn't his son. Ann carried through admirably at first; the people of the church kept saying how well she was holding up, although I tried to help her see that she did not have to put on a show for them and that she could let go.

DR. ALDRICH: The words used to describe someone who doesn't express grief after a loss are usually complimentary, as if it were a good idea not to give in to grief. To say that she came through "admirably" suggests that it would have been less admirable if she had collapsed in a heap, and somebody else had had to take over for her. Although some cultural groups give relatively more sanction to the expression of grief, our society for the most part puts quite a premium on *not* expressing grief or any other kind of feeling. From early childhood the child is encouraged not to be a "baby" but to face adversity with courage. It's done with the best of intentions, but it closes off an important opportunity to prevent further trouble, and it counterbalances your efforts to encourage anyone in Ann's position to express her feelings.

Ann until recently had not expressed her grief. I believe that the delay in the expression of her grief is due to ambivalence. Even though she tries to idealize her son, some of her mixed feelings emerge when she starts her grief work. "He was such a wonderful boy," she says, but along with this feeling comes the thought, "Yes, but he had been drinking, and there were so many other infuriating problems." Ann feels particularly guilty because of the circumstances of his death; her anger about his drinking led to his precipitate ride and the accident. Added to her guilt is shame, since the boy was the product of extramarital relations.

Arthur probably perceived the boy's presence as a constant reproach to his own adequacy as a male. One can easily imagine that there were times when he wished that this boy had never existed. So, when the boy dies, even though the wish to have him gone may have been a relatively small part of his feeling, Arthur also finds it difficult to complete the separation.

The survivor's response to ambivalent feelings about the deceased is not always the same. Ann's response was to conceal her grief entirely and to delay its expression. Arthur's earlier conditioning to ambivalence was probably different; he does not tie the feelings together so closely that he cannot express one without the other. But he seems unable to permit himself to complete his grief work. He acts as though he had to go on grieving indefinitely because to stop expressing grief would be equivalent to being glad that the boy is dead.

This formulation may be somewhat premature, as six months ordinarily is too early to categorize a grief reaction as unduly prolonged; however, Arthur's trip to visit the grave by himself makes me suspect that he is having trouble accepting the boy's death.

MR. ARMSTRONG: I think that Ann is beginning to feel the impact of grief. Until the last two weeks she was active in the choir, but she is no longer able to sing with them. She thinks that if they will not accept her as she is, she does not want to be part of the church. I tell her that everyone has accepted her all along, and that the problem about smoking is the only stumbling block.

DR. ALDRICH: Does she feel that the smoking issue is an excuse to get rid of her? Does she think the rule was made specifically in order to exclude her?

MR. ARMSTRONG: Yes, I think so. I think that she uses the smoking to rationalize their rejection.

DR. ALDRICH: I wonder if her suspicious thinking has gone farther than rationalization. Rationalization means finding an ac-

ceptable reason for thoughts or feelings or behavior. She seems
to be attributing a hostile motivation to the group, and since
there is no evidence that the group actually is hostile to her,
the attribution may be a *projection* of her own anger. With this
pattern, Ann illustrates a third type of response to ambivalent
feelings whose expression cannot be tolerated; grief can be disguised, as well as delayed or prolonged. There are many forms
of disguise; Ann seems to have at least temporarily resolved the
dilemma of her ambivalence by splitting it into its two components and projecting the source of the anger to others. She behaves as if she were saying: "I have only love for my dead son.
I am not angry at him or at anyone else; but the other women
in the choir are angry at me." That is the projection; then the
rationalization—"they are angry at me because of the smoking"
—is tacked onto the projection.

Limited use of projection is reasonably common; but when
its use becomes pervasive and when it cannot be modified by
evidence, it forms the basis of *paranoid* conditions. They are
difficult to manage, in part because it is apparently less disturbing to feel persecuted than to feel guilty and so the projection is hard to overcome, and in part because the counselor may
become the object of the projection and appear to be a perse-
cutor rather than a helper. Ann's view of the choir's reaction
seems close to paranoid, and if her paranoid thinking increases
in scope, she may require psychiatric consultation.

Paranoid thinking, fortunately, is not a common disguise of
grief, but it can occur, and the "impact" you observe may represent the beginning of the manifestation of grief in disguise
rather than its direct expression. I think you should proceed
cautiously with Ann until you can appraise the extent of her
projection. From what we know so far, however, her use of
projection seems relatively limited in degree, and I think you
will be able to help her.

CLERGYMAN 1: Does a bereaved person have to express grief
to a second party, or can he maintain a relatively calm facade

and still have a healthy grief reaction by acknowledging his emotions only to himself?

DR. ALDRICH: Certainly that's a possibility. A person may grieve by himself—he may appear to be avoiding grief by pulling himself together when the pastor calls and then collapsing in a heap when the pastor leaves. In this way a normal grief reaction may exist beneath a "brave" facade. Even so, you may wonder why he does not feel that he can acknowledge even the existence of his grief to his pastor.

CHAPLAIN NIGHSWONGER: Ironically, the teachings of the church may make it hard for someone to share ambivalent feelings with a pastor. We teach people to love and honor their parents and to turn the other cheek. The parishioner often believes not only that he should never show anger but that he should never have any angry feelings at all. Even if he is aware of some of them, he dares not reveal them to his pastor, who is the church's representative.

DR. ALDRICH: We have to look at ourselves as well: there may be something in our approach that makes a grieving person want to protect us from his feelings. Some doctors are made so uncomfortable by open expression of feeling that their patients feel obliged to protect them, and I imagine the same applies to some of the clergy. In addition, there are some cultures that put a tremendous value on stoicism, and the lack of open response may be related to such cultural factors.

CLERGYMAN 2: I want people to feel free to express their grief with me because it's helpful and important. But so often they aren't able to do it, and in spite of my efforts to help them express grief, they keep trying to cover their real feelings. Sometimes I wonder if there's something about my own personality that stops them, but at the same time I know that people generally can bring their other problems to me and share them with me. So I wonder if they have the misconception that grief represents a weakness of faith. They seem to be afraid that if they tell me honestly how badly they feel about their loss, I will reprimand them for having too little faith.

CLERGYMAN 3: The church compounds this problem. When we talk about resurrection and eternal life, we imply that there shouldn't be much grief. Some people do seem to inhibit their expression of grief because they think it is evidence of lack of faith. Then we turn around and tell them they should express their grief. What grief? They are a little confused, and perhaps I am too.

CHAPLAIN NIGHSWONGER: The church has compounded the problem because it too often emphasizes the promise of eternal life, so that indirectly and unintentionally the bereaved get the impression that they ought not to be sad over the loss. Thus grief feelings are inhibited rather than supported in their expression.

DR. ALDRICH: I think we have to make a distinction between what is happening to the person who dies and what is happening to the survivors. Belief in eternal life is reassuring about the fate of the person who dies; however, although part of grief represents concern about how much the deceased will miss because he did not live longer, the more significant part is, I believe, the survivor's feeling of loss, as he mourns for the emptiness in his own life. To some extent we even mourn for someone who leaves on a long trip, although we know that person will be having a pleasant vacation and there is reasonable assurance of a reunion before too long.

CLERGYMAN 4: Grief, then, need not be put into the structure of faith or unfaith? The bereaved feel guilty not because they don't believe in the dead person's immortality but because, as you said earlier, at some time they have wished the other person dead, and now that wish is fulfilled?

DR. ALDRICH: Yes, that's the way it appears to me.

CLERGYMAN 5: But my problem is that I am not willing to let him go and be glad that he's gone, since it's good for him. I am more concerned about myself than about him.

CHAPLAIN NIGHSWONGER: Is it really selfish to acknowledge what the death of a person means to you? Isn't it a reaffirmation of love for that person?

CLERGYMAN 6: Sometimes we fail to indicate that there are interests in self that are perfectly proper, according to the Scriptures.

DR. ALDRICH: Yes, when you say, "Love thy neighbor as thyself," it means that you love yourself as well.

CLERGYMAN 6: Are you now the minister or are you the psychiatrist?

DR. ALDRICH: I guess I am trying to sound like both at once. But there is a good deal of similarity between our ideas at times, both with respect to the patient or parishioner and with respect to ourselves.

We should not forget that both the doctor and the pastor mourn the loss of a patient or parishioner, as they do that of any other friend. This feeling to some extent interferes with their ability to offer help to the survivor. There is an added component to the doctor's grief, because his job is to cure people; if his patient is dead, regardless of how incurable the illness, the doctor didn't do his job. The patient's death seems almost a reproach to the doctor, and this feeling is part of the reason that doctors sometimes develop rather hard shells to protect themselves. The minister does not face this problem, and it may therefore be easier for him to help the survivors.

CLERGYMAN 5: One of our problems is the person who suddenly turns on us and says, "Why did God let this happen to me?" The grief crisis becomes a time when he loses faith. You can't reason with people at a time like that, but keeping quiet doesn't seem to help them either.

CHAPLAIN NIGHSWONGER: This illustration fits into Dr. Aldrich's concept of grief. Your parishioner asks, "Why did God let this happen to me?" not "Why did God let this person go on to his reward?" If you pick up first on the "me," on the loss to him as a person instead of his anger at God for letting it happen, I think you are more likely to help him.

DR. ALDRICH: So do I. In that way, if he is ambivalent toward the person who has died, and if he is shifting or displacing some of his anger onto God whom he sees as unjust, your help with his grief will eventually help him with his faith. You don't have to panic at the threat to his relationship with God and with the church; instead, you can use this question as a signal that he first needs help with his grief.

On the other hand, I don't mean that you should treat his complaint about God's justice lightly, or assume that his anger is necessarily displaced and is not basically directed at God. His question may really be, "Why did God deprive this innocent child of life?" In that case, it may be hard to help him, because you represent God; if he is angry at God, he is also angry at you. Since you didn't cause his loss, you may resent his unfair attack, and it is a temptation to tell him that he is not supposed to be angry at God. But if you, a pastor, can accept his anger and rage at a God who hasn't prolonged the life of his loved one, you show that you can tolerate these feelings; if he can express them to you, he can then perhaps risk communicating his grief and other disturbing feelings.

CLERGYMAN 2: I am worried about some people who feel so hostile toward the church in this situation that they leave, and we don't have a chance to help them.

CHAPLAIN NIGHSWONGER: Perhaps this is when a pastoral call is most important, if we are prepared to tolerate a hostile attack.

DR. ALDRICH: I think you may be right. But it is hard to help someone when you are the target of his displaced hostility. This may be the case with Ann, who seems to have become a destructive influence in her church. She is miserable, but she makes others miserable too. She is so controlling that it is difficult to work with her, and I suspect that she reacts to her minister as if he were another husband whom she can manipulate. It is hard to help her through her grief reaction if you have to worry about keeping her hooks from getting too far into you.

In order to help Ann you've got to be firm and you've got to set some kind of limits to her manipulation and to the side issues she brings up. You may have to say firmly: "I think we can defer the discussion about the memorial tablet and about whether you should smoke here or there. Let's do the first job first. We've got a lot of talking to do about your feelings about your son because I think his death is upsetting you more than you realize. I would like to have you come into my office, where we have an ashtray, and sit down for a while and talk about this." She needs someone to take charge at this point to help her stop flailing around, someone who is not going to respond to her rage with rage of his own and who is not going to give in to her manipulation. If you are firm, you help her to feel that things are not out of control. Although she prefers to talk about everything else but her son, you must keep her talking about him and help her really express her feelings. In this way, you have a fighting chance of helping her.

But you have to be able to tolerate her hostility without fighting back or being defensive, without doing anything about it but recognizing it. It is also important not to be afraid of her. If you are afraid of her, you are in trouble because then you will either fight back or defend yourself; the fight will tend to become the focus of the communication between you. She will probably test you to find out how far she can manipulate you, but when she finds that you are firm and that you are in charge, she will begin to get to work on her grief.

CLERGYMAN 5: I frequently encourage people to express their grief, but sometimes I am not sure that I am being of service to them. As pastors, we are in a delicate position; our parishioners need to maintain their self-esteem in our presence. They see us as critics, not as counselors, and they have to show us evidence of their ability to control their lives. When I have tried to push beyond their outward calm, to dig in and get them really to open up, I have often worried about going too far. You seem to encourage this kind of directive approach, however, instead of the nondirective (Rogerian) approach I thought psychiatrists recommended.

DR. ALDRICH: Nondirective counseling is an appealing technique because it seems so easy to undertake. Much of it is based on the assumption that if you simply listen to the client and occasionally reflect his feelings, he will do the rest. Psychiatrists differ in their opinions about it, and I can only give you my own view. I think it's a useful technique in some counseling situations, but it is not appropriate to all situations. Rather than using one approach indiscriminately, counselors should adapt their technique to the specific client and to the specific problem under consideration.

I think nondirective counseling is particularly inappropriate in dealing with a short-term problem in a person whose previous level of functioning was reasonably good. Even when it was not so good, the nondirective approach may encourage people to open up more than the counselor can handle. The more directive approach digs in, as you say, but it also limits somewhat the scope of the digging. In a grief reaction, the counselor focuses on the grief and its implications, which usually are fairly close to the surface.

I recognize that your parishioners have more need to maintain their self-esteem with you than our patients have with us, but I think this facet of counseling can be managed, both through your attitude and your words. Sometimes before you get to the grief, you have to talk about their need to protect themselves in your presence, and their perception of you as critical. You might say something like this:

"You seem to be trying hard to keep your feelings in check when you're talking with me. I wonder if you're afraid that I would disapprove if you really expressed them. You hear me preaching so often about God's love and the eternal life that you may think that I will preach to you and imply that you shouldn't feel so badly about your loss."

Don't spoil it by prematurely reassuring her that you wouldn't preach; that would cut off her response, because she would think that you were making allowances for the situation and that you really did believe that she shouldn't feel badly. Let her deny it or acknowledge it; if she denies it, she is likely to be responding conventionally, and you can then help her best by saying, "Well, it sometimes is hard to share feelings you may be a little embarrassed about with someone who seems to set himself up as a judge every Sunday morning."

She may still deny it, but you've made your point, that you can understand her reticence about showing feelings in your presence, and you can go on to make a distinction between her feelings about the deceased and the hereafter and her feelings about herself and the loss she feels now. If she does acknowledge her concern, you must again try to understand rather than reassure. If you say, "I can see that it's difficult," she senses that you understand how she feels about you and she can anticipate that you will understand how she feels about others. This is more effective than simply *telling* her that you will understand.

Working with the ambivalence of the bereaved requires a gradual approach. Obviously, you would not say to someone like Ann, "Although you are telling yourself that you loved your son, you really hated him." Instead, you recognize her feeling of loss and encourage her to tell you about their shared experiences through the years. She may begin with an idealized picture, but she will eventually run short of idealizations; then, perhaps with the gentlest nudge from you, she will begin to tell some of the incidents in which everything was not perfect. The nudge may be a question, such as, "How did he respond to discipline?" You take your cue from the response and try to help her go at her own pace.

In Ann's case, the association of the drinking episode with her son's death might seem a natural point of departure; nevertheless it is wiser not to focus on the negative side of the ambivalence at first. Mr. Armstrong would still gradually work through her positive feelings until she could begin to accept the negative; at this point he might comment, in the form of a half-finished sentence, "You felt awfully unhappy about his drinking. . . ." She might say, "I felt so inadequate because I couldn't do anything about it." He could then say, "It must have been pretty frustrating. . . ." And out of that, you see, can come gradual acceptance of her anger since Mr. Armstrong's attitude indicates that he can accept her resentment of the boy, even though he is dead, and even though she doesn't specifically state it. Your attitude that it is all right to be resentful as well as loving of family members, living or dead, slowly gets across.

The expression and resolution of grief reasonably soon after the loss is a crucial factor in the prevention of later mental illness. I have discussed grief at some length, therefore, because

I believe that helping bereaved parishioners express their grief is about the most significant way in which the clergyman can contribute to mental health. You don't want to make people feel guilty or ashamed for not expressing grief; but as you talk with them about their feelings, you can give them sanction for expressing their grief, either with you or in the privacy of their own homes.

CHAPLAIN NIGHSWONGER: Perhaps we can help people express grief not only through the counseling relationship but from the pulpit as we speak of grief and loss in sermons. If we can anticipate grief for our congregations in an educational or inspirational way, people will have some built-in understanding and expectations when a loss does occur, and will feel more free to express their feelings.

DR. ALDRICH: Such an atmosphere may also encourage adults to help their children express grief. Most children can tolerate the loss of a mother or father, but too often they are misled about the reality of the parent's death, or they are made to feel so ashamed of their grief that all their feelings are bottled up at the time. These feelings may emerge later in the guise of an emotional disturbance.

CLERGYMAN 4: Is there a similar problem for a child whose parents divorce?

DR. ALDRICH: Yes, and a loss like that is often more difficult to mourn than a death.

CLERGYMAN 4: Because if a person isn't dead, there is always a chance that he will return?

DR. ALDRICH: That is part of it. But also the child may feel responsible for the separation and he usually feels rejected. He thinks, "If father had really loved me, he would have stayed."

In addition, he may resent father's leaving and may feel guilty about this resentment, since in the past he probably at some time has wished that his father would somehow disappear and not interfere with his relationship with his mother. In view of the connotations of this wish, particularly as a death wish, it usually is not permitted to remain in consciousness because it makes the child feel so guilty. However, anger toward a parent who deserts is usually easier to mobilize than anger toward a parent who dies; and once the anger is expressed, the process of mourning can begin.

Most people with grief reactions can be helped relatively easily, and it's nice to feel that you are accomplishing something in these cases; counseling work can often be discouraging. Ann's case may be somewhat difficult, because she seems to have been in some trouble all along and her grief represents the most recent incident in an accumulation of problems. But by focusing on her grief as the most immediate problem, you may be able to help her regain her previous, somewhat precarious, balance, which would be no small achievement.

Chapter Three

ANXIETY
AND
DEPRESSION

Mr. Benson's parishioner, Bea, suffers from persistent long-term anxiety and depression, which are disguised in a variety of ways. The problems Bea complains of are related to her dissatisfaction with her social role. The case shows how the clergyman can help his parishioner accept herself and her own angry feelings by demonstrating that he can accept her as a whole person.

MR. BENSON: Bea is a married woman in her mid-twenties who has three children: a daughter four, and sons six and two. She complains of periods of depression that make her want to stay in bed in the morning. I think she stays in bed not because she likes to but because she doesn't want to face anything else. She has a general feeling of apprehensiveness most of her waking time, a feeling that something terrible may happen. She is also abnormally concerned about any physical irregularity; for example, she became very upset about a slight ear infection and was convinced she would lose her hearing even after she had been reassured by her physician.

Besides her general apprehensiveness, Bea is obsessed with a fear that she will have to go to the toilet and will not be able to get there. She becomes panicky if she sits in church in a place from which it would be embarrassing to get up during the service, or if she feels, at a party or at the theater, that she couldn't get to the toilet without people noticing her. This fear occurs in spite of the fact that she cannot remember any incident when she actually was embarrassed by having to go to the toilet. She also tells me of a frequent dream in which a mattress is coming down on her, and her only protection is a straight pin.

She is an unusually attractive young woman, and her husband is quite plain-looking. He is shy, but very few things seem to satisfy him. He constantly complains, about the children, about their finances, about everything. Bea speaks of him with great appreciation and little open hostility. Although her apartment is tastefully furnished, she feels inadequate and gets upset when friends or family come in for dinner or a little party. She often avoids social situations and has canceled engagements because the feeling of inadequacy sweeps over her. But she is also highly competitive about homemaking, dress, and looks, and is jealous of her husband's attention to other women, though she says he has never given her any cause for her jealousy.

Bea was an only child. Her father was a domineering man who preferred boys and encouraged her to show masculine traits, so that she tried to compete with boys in sports. Her mother constantly warned Bea to watch out for the father and to placate him. Bea tried to please him, and at the same time resented him. When she returned late from a high school dance, her father embarrassed her so much by reprimanding her in front of her boyfriend that she switched schools in order to avoid facing her friends.

For about a year and a half after her marriage, Bea was happy. After the first baby came, her symptoms began, and they have grown steadily worse. She and her husband are now both desperately afraid of another pregnancy. They express love for their children, but they also express, at least to me, great resentment at being cooped up in the house in order to take care of them.

Bea has developed a sense of almost compulsive loyalty to the church and a compulsive feeling about religion. She feels that she *has* to do various things to please God. She fears God, I think, in some sort of identification with her father.

Soon after I came to the church, I dropped in to talk with Bea and her husband. In front of him, she asked for an appointment to talk with me in my office. After seeing her, I talked with her doctor. He told me that he had not been able to find any physical illness and agreed with my impression that her relationship with her father was the dominant cause of her troubles.

Since then, I have been counseling her at weekly intervals, but I'm not sure I'm on the right track. I get worried about her; my predecessor was called to their home once or twice because she was so upset, and they called me one night when she was almost hysterical.

DR. ALDRICH: I think we should first try to organize what we know about Bea's personality structure, recognizing that in order to do this, we will have to make some assumptions, and that further information may invalidate at least part of the formulation. Even material that she presents as fact may not be accurate, especially if it is about her childhood. I am not suggesting that she is consciously misrepresenting her history, but that either her perception or her recollection, or both, may be inaccurate.

I think we can assume that Bea's father was somewhat insecure in his masculinity; otherwise he would not have had to be so domineering, and he would have been more accepting of female children. When his first child was born, he was probably disappointed. I imagine that when the obstetrician said, "You've got a lovely girl," his face fell, and he went off and had an extra drink or two. This reaction is not unusual and is not particularly troublesome if the mother is strong enough to hold her own in the family. In this family, however, the mother is described as subservient. Women, as her daughter perceived their role, are not only less valuable than men, but weaker. In part as a result of this perception, and perhaps in response to her father's subtle encouragement, Bea made an effort to be like a boy—a tomboy. Behaving as a tomboy, however, is more acceptable in a child than in an adolescent, and it is harder to deny femininity as an adolescent. In adolescence, therefore, she tried to establish a more feminine orientation, and went out with boys, although some of her preference for a male orientation persisted.

You mentioned that Bea is unusually competitive with women. External appearances may be misleading about a woman's acceptance of a feminine orientation. For example, one way for a girl to combat a feeling of inadequacy as a woman is to become the best-dressed woman in town. Later on, she may try to compensate for her feelings of inadequacy as a woman by being unusually competitive with other women in homemaking, becoming perfectionistic about her housekeeping and her children. A woman of this type can be disproportionately upset if one of her children sucks his thumb or something like that. However, external appearances do not always indicate the same underlying cause. For example, it is hard to know whether the university co-ed who runs around in jeans and old tennis shoes is still attempting to identify as a boy, or whether she feels so adequate as a woman that she just doesn't need to demonstrate it.

The search for an identity independent of the family is a significant task for the adolescent; usually, by the time he is nineteen or twenty, he has attained a feeling of identity, with more or less acceptance of his masculinity or femininity. The strength of the identification with his sex that he reaches during adolescence affects his later behavior. For instance, when you come to call on a woman who wears slacks around the house because it is more comfortable, she is likely to say, "Oh, dear me! I look a sight." If she feels terribly embarrassed, runs up to change, and then apologizes for the next half hour, you may suspect that she really feels inadequate as a woman. But if she says, "I'll go up and change," and you say, "Don't bother," and she says, "O.K., I won't bother," or something like that, you get the idea that she probably feels rather adequate as a woman, and that she doesn't need the outer trappings to reassure herself that she's really an A1, feminine, female woman. On the other hand, if she aggressively wears slacks even when they are inappropriate, you are entitled to wonder what she is trying to prove.

Bea may have found it difficult to establish an identity independent of her family because her relationship with her father was so important to her. The possibility that a father can have a crush, as it were, on his daughter is hard for most of us to accept. But it can happen, and in fact, to some extent these feelings are almost universal; a father traditionally considers no suitor adequate for his daughter's hand.

This doesn't necessarily mean that there is an overt sexual attraction between father and daughter; but the relationships between father and daughter and between mother and son are different from those between parents and children of the same sex. The sexual component of the relationship between father and daughter may be revealed in his wish for her to be more like a boy, so that he can be close to her without any sexual overtones. Or it may be manifested in unwarranted concern about his daughter's sexual behavior; often a parental reprimand about staying out too late carries a latent suspicion that there has been some sexual activity. Mothers, too, can be suspicious of their daughters' sexual activity, through identification with their own hidden wishes or fears.

I suspect that Bea's father accused her of sexual activity which, at least to begin with, was only in his mind. The accusation and expectation, however, contribute to their own fulfillment; the best way to produce any kind of behavior in someone else is to let him know that you expect it and assume its presence. The best way to encourage a daughter to get pregnant, therefore, is to accuse her without evidence of having sexual relations. She hears a double message: she should not have intercourse, but at the same time you do not expect her to have the capacity to say "No." The implied assumption that she has no controls reduces her own confidence in her ability to control. As a result, either the behavior is expressed, or she builds up synthetic and unrealistic controls against any expression of the expected behavior in any situation. So parental expectation of sexual misbehavior may contribute to promiscuity, or it may contribute to the opposite, a denial of sexuality which can result in frigidity.

I have been speaking generally and I don't know yet whether this formulation applies to Bea. Is she frigid?

MR. BENSON: She said that sexual relations are normal with normal pleasure.

DR. ALDRICH: I guess I'm a little skeptical about her answer. This skepticism is an occupational characteristic of psychiatrists; it is sometimes annoying because it seems to make the psychiatrist's preconception right, no matter what the patient says! Nevertheless, people are more defensive about their sexual lives than about anything else, and I would be somewhat surprised if, with her background, she had no problems in the sexual area. I'm not sure, however, that you need to try to find this out, at least not at this stage. In any case, there is some evidence that she has had a lot of trouble reconciling herself to the depreciated female role.

CLERGYMAN 6: I don't quite understand. Is her problem really her father or is it her mother?

DR. ALDRICH: It's not that simple: either one or the other. It's a combination of both. A mother she could respect and with whom she could really identify, a mother who didn't give her the message, "You've got to placate Father, and do as he says; I hate him, but we have to do what he says," perhaps could have helped her overcome her father's pressure to take on a more masculine role. To that extent, you can say it is the mother. On the other hand, if her father had been a benign, understanding, and protective person, she might have been all right, or perhaps she might have had a different type of disturbance. So it isn't only one or the other parent; it is the total situation, including a lot of other factors we don't know about.

CLERGYMAN 6: Are you suggesting that specific life experiences can be counted on to lead to specific symptoms? For instance, does pregnancy stir up special feelings toward one parent that result in a particular set of symptoms?

DR. ALDRICH: Again, it's not so simple. The same sequence of events is *likely* to be followed by certain symptoms, but in some people it may produce different symptoms and in others no symptoms. Furthermore, the same symptoms may result from a variety of sequences. It does seem a bit hit or miss at times, but we work on probabilities, and then we are, or should be, careful to check our theories against the evidence. The theory at least gives us an idea of where to look for the evidence.

In contrast to Ann's case [Chapter Two], in which we could see how a specific and fairly well defined problem had recently arisen out of a particular situation, Bea's difficulties are much more diffuse and of longer duration. Unfortunately, Bea's case is also more typical of what you encounter in pastoral work.

CLERGYMAN 4: Theoretically, should it not be possible for her, either with guidance or by herself, to readjust her outlook now that she is happily married and has a husband who plays the male role differently from her father?

DR. ALDRICH: Her attitude toward men cannot change as readily as would be expected from logic alone. She may protect herself from changing her attitude by perceiving her husband as a special case, a man weak enough to be dominated. If she can dominate him, or if she can convince herself that she is dominating him, she can feel safe because she is outdoing a male at his own game.

MR. BENSON: She tells me that she is anxious to know just exactly what he wants from her and how she should react to him.

DR. ALDRICH: She might say that because she is trying to make up for dominating and controlling him. Sometimes a girl who is insecure as a woman, yet recognizes that it is hopeless really to take over the man's role, compromises by entering a marriage in which she can play the dominant role and either work or participate strenuously in the community. This kind of marriage may work out well as long as the wife can maintain this role. Trouble comes when the roles are reversed, as in pregnancy, which pushes the wife into a maternal role so that she has to face all the implications of being a woman like her mother. She must now take care of the baby while her husband goes out to work and has an interesting and presumably more significant life with other people. She can no longer compensate for her envy of the male or of the male's role. She can no longer act a masculine part, the part that gained acceptance (or protection) from father. She has become a drudge, which she hates and resents; but because it is bad and dangerous to resent it, she has become depressed and anxious. In Bea's case, a sign of depression is her tendency to stay in bed in the morning; the morning is, for reasons we don't understand, the worst time of day for a patient with a severe depression. Her anxiety may reflect her apprehension that unconscious anger might break through into consciousness and, therefore, into action.

I suspect that Bea resents deeply both her children and her husband, because their presence obliges her to play a feminine role; but she cannot acknowledge the extent of her resentment, even to herself. Her anxiety in response to these current resentments is complicated by anxiety in response to resentments that date back to her mother and father.

The symptoms she discussed with the pastor represent her attempts to deal with the anxiety. One of the mechanisms, for instance, is displacement of the apparent source of her anxiety to a part of her body; after the ear infection served to focus her anxiety on her ear, she feared despite reassurance that she was becoming deaf.

CLERGYMAN 2: This is where I have trouble in my own work. When I believe that I understand a person's problem, I still cannot bring him to an emotional recognition and acceptance. I feel that I just do not know enough to help. I usually put it in the form of a suggestion—"Have you ever thought you might be afraid of your anger?"—and that sort of thing, but it is still verbalization and intellectualization rather than realization.

DR. ALDRICH: This is a tough problem for all of us. I'm not sure I can improve on your response, and it may be more helpful than you think. By your suggestion you are conveying an acceptance of her and of her anger; this is helpful even if she denies that there is any anger to fear.

If all we had to do was to tell people the meaning of their symptoms, our lives would be much simpler and psychiatrists would be out of a job. But translating from intellectual understanding to emotional acceptance is difficult. It seems to require, in Alexander's terms, a "corrective emotional experience"; by this he meant reliving the disturbing emotions, that were initially experienced in a hostile or rejecting or too seductive relationship, in the context of a therapeutic, more accepting relationship. Therefore, rather than attempting to convey to the patient an intellectual understanding of his problems, therapists generally try to help him experience a different and more realistic emotional response to the kind of situation that seems to be contributing to the problems. For example, I wouldn't bluntly tell Bea, "You hate being a woman." Instead, I would perhaps start with a half-sentence such as, "This all seems to have started around the time when . . . ," and I would expect her to finish my sentence by saying, "with my first pregnancy." Then I would ask her, "Could you tell me more about how you were feeling when you discovered you were pregnant?" She would probably tell me about her job and how she liked it, and then how she felt when she was first pregnant. From experience with similar cases, I would expect to hear that she felt fine, because now she was going to prove herself in woman's childbearing role, as well as in a job. I'd then ask when the letdown came, and what she thought might have caused her to become depressed or anxious. I wouldn't expect her to know, but I'd want her to think about it; I would want to know what the depression and anxiety meant to her, and I would encourage her to tell me more about them and their effects on her functioning in her home and as a mother.

I would not try to reassure her by telling her she is a good mother, because I would be afraid that she would only become more depressed. But by my attitude of interest in her feminine aspect, I would try to correct her feeling that a male authority on whom she depends, someone in a father role, could not possibly accept a daughter and would much rather have a son. I would also try to correct her feeling that someone in a father role could not accept her sexuality. I am assuming, from her history and from my experience with similar patients, that an important cause of her troubles is the breakdown of her attempt to act a man's role, a breakdown that results in part from the inescapable reality that motherhood forces on her. I would try to help her correct the earlier emotional experience that reduced her self-esteem as a woman, and I would also try to help her correct the fear of consequences that made her unable to let herself feel resentful. In order to do all this, she has to put me in the role of a father-person, which spontaneously occurs in most instances because of the paternal social role of the physician or pastor. She transfers her father's attitudes to me, and then can discover that what was true of her father is not inevitably true of all men.

She makes this discovery gradually, and to help her I have to be a person who can tolerate her anger without being upset. In our sessions I neither encourage nor discourage the expression of her anger; I just recognize it, and let her see that it doesn't upset me. In that way she becomes less scared of her anger. I also let her perceive that I do not think she will kill or hurt anybody if she gets angry.

I think Bea has hidden her angry feelings from herself for so long that she does not realize she can look at them without having to express them directly. Little by little, as she lets herself see and acknowledge the anger that is inside her, and as she finds that I am not scared of it, she becomes less scared of it. This technique does not mean that I let her break up my furniture. It would frighten her even more if I did so. She needs to find out that she can *be* angry without *doing* anything about it. She can *say* anything she wants to me even if it's unfair; if it is unfair, and she recognizes and feels ashamed of it, I try to help her gain confidence in her capacity to determine when the expression of anger is appropriate and when inappropriate.

The goal of Bea's treatment is her gradual acceptance of repressed anger, and it can be accomplished through a corrective emotional experience with someone who resembles key people in her background but who responds differently. I respond differently in that I accept her as a woman, as an angry woman and as a sexual woman, without getting upset. Once she discovers that it is possible for me to accept her hidden self, she can begin to accept her hidden self and to adapt more realistically.

Adapting more realistically includes accepting her interests outside the home and becoming somewhat less perfectionistic about housekeeping and child care. I have a similar patient who has now decided to get a housekeeper for her children and go back to work. Until now she has felt ashamed of wanting to return to work, insisting that all women should stay home and take care of their children, even if they are more interested in working. As she discovered in treatment that I was not critical of her, as her mother was, for her resentment at being tied down at home, she began to permit herself at least to consider an alternative. She has felt guilty about her resentment of her father and her husband, who go off each morning to do all sorts of interesting things while she and her mother are stuck at home. She also has felt guilty about her resentment of her children, who keep her tied down at home. As she has repeatedly found that I don't criticize or condemn her for these resentments, she has finally let herself think, "Maybe all of us would be better off if I returned to work."

I have not attempted to modify her character structure; I have not said to her, "You've got to change yourself completely and be a woman who likes to be a housewife." That might be a goal of psychoanalysis, but not of psychotherapy or counseling. Instead, I say: "I can accept you as a woman who needs the sense of competence that a certain amount of competition with men provides. You can be a woman and do this too. You don't have to feel guilty or ashamed."

Here is where the old middle-class social morality gets in women's way. People think women *ought* to stay at home and take care of their children. As a general rule, I would agree, but it is not always true. I believe that this woman is better off at work and her children are better off having her at work. She can find a housekeeper who will enjoy taking care of her home and children. When she comes home in the evening, she will be much more comfortable with the children and much less resentful after the gratification of a day at the office. The goal of treatment is to relieve her of the guilt that keeps her locked in the house. I don't think Bea necessarily should be encouraged to go to work, but acceptance of some of her resentment can help both her anxiety and her depression.

Although I have been discussing psychotherapy as I would undertake it, I think that it has much in common with the technique of pastoral counseling.

CLERGYMAN 7: Perhaps I am being too psychoanalytic, but is her fear of people seeing her going to the toilet related to a castration complex?

DR. ALDRICH: How do you mean?

CLERGYMAN 7: As I understand it, in a family in which boys are favored, a girl may feel that, because of her anatomical differences, she is a less competent or complete person.

DR. ALDRICH: According to psychoanalytic theory, this response originates in the developmental period in which family rivalry occurs, from around three to six, as the child begins to comprehend the full significance of the difference between boys and girls. The idea of "castration" and its anatomical implications is usually perceived more in a symbolic than a literal sense. In this case, a domineering father to whom the mother resentfully gave in may have created a background against which the daughter will find it difficult to enjoy the prospect of adult femininity. She feels ashamed of her femininity, and symbolically ashamed of her lack of the male organ, which is both reproductive and excretory in its function. This shame therefore may well be associated with her fear of not making it to the toilet. It may have to do not only with other people observing her going to the toilet but also with her observation of herself and her feeling about her genitals, about what is missing.

If she were being psychoanalyzed, this interpretation might be made at an appropriate time in the analysis. In less intensive psychotherapy or in counseling, I would listen to her concern about the toilet but not focus on it directly. I would let sleeping dogs lie, as far as its meaning is concerned, because it goes back too far and the symbolism is too deeply unconscious to work with in this kind of treatment. As she becomes more reconciled to herself as a woman, this symptom will probably become less pervasive.

CLERGYMAN 7: What about the dream of protecting herself from the descending mattress with the pin? Would you say that the pin is symbolic of the penis, and that she needs it to protect herself from being overcome? Or should we be trying to interpret dreams with our training?

DR. ALDRICH: An attempt to interpret dreams in any kind of treatment short of psychoanalysis or intensive psychotherapy in experienced hands is likely to be neither accurate nor productive, and it can even be harmful. In any case, more information about Bea and about her associations to the dream would be necessary before trying to interpret it. Your idea about it may be right: the pin and the descending mattress may well combine her wish to be male and her guilt about the wish. But regardless of the dream's meaning, I don't think it is necessary or even advisable to explore her specifically sexual concerns. She has not asked for help in this area; any sexual concerns are buried, if indeed they exist, and you have enough to do to help her gain self-esteem as a woman and to strengthen her ego.

CLERGYMAN 7: If you stay away from all that, how do you ever find out what really happened to her? Don't you have to find out at some point?

DR. ALDRICH: No, as a matter of fact, you don't. This is a point that is often misunderstood. Freud developed much of his theoretical material from the memories of his patients. With his help, they could remember various disturbing things that apparently had happened in their childhood but that they had forgotten. Freud, however, was not content to accept everything at face value; he checked up and discovered that some of the things his patients "remembered" couldn't possibly have happened. A lesser man might have said at this point, "Well, it looks as if my theory is shot, and I will forget the whole thing." But Freud continued to study these "memories," and began to realize that the actual past is not as significant as the way the past is perceived.

Regardless of what her father was really like, Bea responded to her perception of him. As she becomes emancipated from him or from her perception of him, his real or imagined opinions will matter less to her. Emancipation can be carried out through the corrective emotional experience in counseling, and does not require the uncovering of all her unconscious feelings and attitudes. Furthermore, once Bea frees herself from some of her past attitudes, she may be able to repress much of her remaining anger. She may even be much more tolerant of her father than she was before and she can begin to see him in a broader context.

Don't get the idea that because it is a defense mechanism, repression is undesirable; repression is the mechanism of civilization, and we all need to use it to some extent. If you can help Bea strengthen her defenses and repress better, you have done a good job. That would be my goal with her, and I would not want to unearth too much or try to remake her into a completely contented housewife. I would consider her care a success if she could accept some of her anger and overcome some of her feeling of inadequacy. In that way she could be more relaxed as a woman and, incidentally, could make it easier for her daughter to grow up feeling that it is all right to be a woman.

Chapter Four

SUICIDE
RISK

The pastor's assessment of a suicide risk determines his decision to make a referral or to continue with the case himself. One aspect of the psychiatric consultant's role is to provide guidance in making this diagnosis accurately and in understanding the background of the suicidal impulse. In Mr. Cook's case, the origin of Chris's suicide impulse is related to his unexpressed anger at his father's suicide.

MR. COOK: Chris is thirty-one years old, married, with a three-year-old daughter. A few weeks ago he asked me to have lunch to discuss something that he chose to call a problem about religion. The previous week, his wife had asked to see me, so far as I know without his knowledge. She was quite upset about him, complaining that he was financially irresponsible, had changed jobs a number of times, and now had two jobs so that he was seldom at home. She also complained that he was non-communicative and had nothing to do with her sexually.

Chris is the kind of person who calls on me intermittently and then drops out of the picture completely for months; this is the pattern in his contacts with other resources, including his doctor. At lunch he wanted primarily to tell me that he thought his father had committed suicide out of high and holy motives, in response to the Scriptural injunction, "If thy right eye offend thee, pluck it out."

74

His father had committed suicide when Chris was fifteen. Chris said he could easily believe his father had concluded that he was the problem in the home, although he really wasn't, and that he had committed suicide to save the family. Without making verbal connection between the two problems, Chris then told me about a movie he had recently seen, in which one of the characters sacrificed himself to prevent a greater tragedy. He was quite impressed with the reasonableness of this solution.

I may be forcing the issue in relating the two, but I thought it was possible that he applied both the experience of his father and the theme of the movie to himself. I am concerned about a possible suicide risk and I feel that he may need more help than I can give. If so, how do I refer him? It is hard for me to persuade him to get help; I have already made an unsuccessful effort to refer him to a family service agency. I really think he ought to go to a psychiatric clinic.

His mother is a quiet, hard-working person who is active in our church. He has two younger brothers and a younger sister . . .

Dr. Aldrich: How old is she?

Mr. Cook: The sister is about sixteen. Why do you ask?

Dr. Aldrich: I wanted to find out whether she was the same age at the time of the father's suicide as Chris's daughter is now. If Chris closely identifies with the father, he might become depressed at a time in his life which corresponds to the time when his father became depressed. If his sister is sixteen and he is thirty-one and the father's suicide occurred when he was fifteen, his sister's birth and his father's death were close together. I would want to know whether there was some relationship between the two events, and also how old the father was when he died. Of course, it may turn out that the dates Chris recalls are inaccurate.

MR. COOK: The two were closely related. The suicide was either shortly before or shortly after the sister's birth, and the father was the same age that Chris is now.

After his father's suicide, my parishioner was in a mental hospital for a while. He is very noncommunicative about that episode. About five years ago he married a girl named Cathy whose parents are divorced. Her mother lives in the upstairs apartment. Chris and the mother blame each other for Cathy's troubles; she calls him an irresponsible husband, and he calls her a mother who has no love and no ability to inspire confidence. She told him she was going to a third party, presumably a counselor, to settle it; he assumed that she was going to try to have him committed.

If it were not for Chris's suicide hint, I would be equally concerned about Cathy. She feels completely unloved by both her mother and her husband and troubled about her relationship with her daughter. The grandmother gives the child anything she wants; Cathy feels that she herself has to do all the disciplining whereas her mother does all the giving.

Chris attends another church every Sunday because he feels that he is not accepted in his own church. He thinks his opinions are too controversial, so he goes to a different church where he can speak out because he doesn't care what the people think; he doesn't want to upset his own church where his mother attends.

CHAPLAIN NIGHSWONGER: You mentioned that Chris had sought to reconcile his father's suicide on a religious basis. How would you describe his religious attitudes?

MR. COOK: He talks in religious terminology and he attends Bible discussion groups and any classes that give him a chance to sound off. He makes provocative and unconventional interpretations of Scriptural passages and seems to enjoy taking a position opposite to the preacher's.

Cathy does not go to church at all. I am their pastor, however, and she calls on me for counseling.

DR. ALDRICH: The wife's initial complaint was that he was financially irresponsible, and yet he had two jobs and was working so hard that he did not have time for any of the amenities of domestic life.

MR. COOK: His jobs are irregular but his bills are consistently high because he buys everything he wants and dresses quite extravagantly. He acknowledges that her complaints are justified; on the surface he agrees that he hasn't accomplished what he should have accomplished, and that he hasn't fulfilled his responsibilities. He says, however, that if she will give him time, he will work it out; he claims that it's really a religious problem.

CHAPLAIN NICHSWONGER: How does he make the financial problem into a religious problem?

MR. COOK: It's his confusion of values. He says he's got to think through his philosophy of life and he is now making progress on it. This is the way he talks with me, and I'm afraid, or I hesitate, to give him the answers I want to give and to tell him that these are symptoms, not religious problems.

DR. ALDRICH: How long has this been going on?

MR. COOK: I don't know about the exact circumstances, but he has followed the same pattern at church for a long time. I had not heard from his wife until recently. He has never characterized his troubles as marital problems. On the other hand, Cathy says that any kind of sexual contact between them has been very rare ever since they were married; in fact, any kind of communication about what they're doing is rare.

DR. ALDRICH: In a way it is reassuring that there has not been a dramatic personality change in Chris; he is really about the same as he has always been. That is why I asked how long the problem has been going on. If he had been a communicative, sexually well-adjusted, financially responsible fellow up to a certain time and then had gradually started going downhill, I would be more worried because this kind of personality change tends to progress. But if he has been functioning indefinitely at this level and has not undergone any marked deterioration, it suggests a character disorder, a fixation at a developmental level rather than a regression.

The duration of a problem is quite important. If a problem is of relatively short duration, it is usually more amenable to treatment; if it is insidiously and slowly progressive, it is likely to keep on going in spite of anything you can do. If it is a static problem due to fixation at an earlier developmental stage, as Chris's seems to be, it is more difficult to treat but not so likely to become worse.

The same applies to a marital problem. If it has gone on since the beginning of the marriage, I'm pessimistic about what can be done, because there is no plateau to go back to. On the other hand, if the marriage was originally in good shape and has fallen apart for some particular reason, the chances of putting it back together are better.

Chris's wife says that there has been trouble all along, but I wonder if there was a change when the daughter was born? If Chris is identifying with his father, he may have been depressed ever since her birth. His extravagant clothes may represent a defense against depression, an attempt to cover it up.

The marriage has gone on for five years, and the daughter is three; you are not going to do any harm by asking, "Could you tell me what the marriage was like at the very beginning, and how it differed then from the way it is now?" People can often describe other people or events better if you ask for a comparison rather than a direct explanation. For example, if a woman says, "My husband is a wonderful person," and you say, "How do you mean?" it may be hard for her to find words other than "Well, he is just wonderful." To help her be more specific, you might say, "Could you compare him, for example, with your brother or your father?" Then she might say something like, "Well, he is more fussy and more perfectionistic than my father, who was more easygoing." You begin to get a picture of both —two for the price of one. It's the same way with time; a question such as "Could you compare the marriage in its first year, before the child was born, with the way the marriage worked out after the child came?" is likely to elicit more useful information than separate questions about two given points in time.

CLERGYMAN 8: Isn't this fellow quite evasive? From what we've heard so far, he hasn't shared much of his problem.

DR. ALDRICH: I doubt that he trusts anybody enough to share much with them, which makes any intervention on your part more difficult.

CHAPLAIN NIGHSWONGER: I wonder whether Chris came to you for help on his own initiative. Someone else in the family, his wife or his mother-in-law, may have wanted him to see you. He ties your hands with problems that are difficult for the pastor to handle, such as his father's suicide and his religious interpretation of it, and stays clear of other things.

DR. ALDRICH: He certainly tried hard to define his problem in terms far removed from day-to-day living.

CLERGYMAN 1: Don't you think that his appearance so soon after his wife's visit is more than a coincidence?

MR. COOK: They both assured me that he just happened to come at that time, but even so I believe that he may have come in response to pressure. Talking with me may have encouraged Cathy to put more pressure on him. As a matter of fact, a year ago they went together to see their family physician who is also a member of my congregation. According to Cathy, the doctor said that Chris was at fault because he wasn't an adequate husband, and that she was entitled to a divorce. Chris said that he felt the doctor had not been helpful; and besides, the doctor had sent him a bill when Chris had just talked with him as a Christian.

DR. ALDRICH: That's a problem you people don't have.

CHAPLAIN NIGHSWONGER: It's also a compensation we don't have.

DR. ALDRICH: Often a wife or husband projects the whole responsibility for a marital problem onto the spouse; in such a situation, regardless of how you handle it, you will be reported to have said that the problem is all the spouse's fault and that the spouse is the one who needs help. Even a question can be interpreted as evidence of taking sides. After I have listened to a wife's long bill of particulars against her husband, I may ask, "Have you considered separation?" She says, "Oh, no, I couldn't for the children's sake (or for religion's sake, or for some other kind of sake)." Later I am quoted as having *recommended* separation, when all I've asked is whether she has *considered* it. So I am always skeptical of secondhand reports that a doctor has recommended divorce. These are seldom conscious distortions; generally, people simply listen to what they want to hear, and often what they want to hear is support for an attack on the marital partner.

Perhaps at this point we should summarize. We have been discussing the importance of finding out whether Chris's financial irresponsibility, his uncommunicativeness, and his sexual abstinence have been present throughout the marriage, or whether they have a more recent onset. We have considered the possibility that, since his father apparently committed suicide about the time that a daughter was born, Chris's daughter's birth might have triggered his own suicidal thoughts, particularly since he seems to identify with his father so much. We know that he is concerned about his father's suicide, about the movie story of sacrifice, and about the Biblical passage concerning retaliation. We also know that his father died when Chris was an adolescent.

It is bad enough to lose a father in any way at any time, but it happened to Chris in the worst way at the worst time. In adolescence, emotional ties to other people become physiologically or sexually supercharged, and a new kind of competitiveness appears. The adolescent boy is another man in the family. He wants to be an adult; he wants to show that he can drive the car as well as the old man can. Competition includes both sexual and aggressive elements; the adolescent's ability to manage the aggressive element depends upon the extent to which he has been able to express his angry feelings and see them in realistic perspective. If he has never felt free to express them, his competitiveness may become invested with a magical destructiveness.

If an adolescent's aggression gets to the point where he feels like knocking the old man off his perch, and just then the old man falls off his perch, all the boy's internal fantasies and wishes about taking over the role of authority come true. In Chris's case he became the "father" of the family, since he was the oldest boy. He had just what he wanted, but he had it because his father had destroyed himself. If Chris felt that his hostility contributed to his father's death, he could have been talking about himself when he said if the eye offends, pluck it out; he could believe that he deserves the same fate as his father, having destroyed him and taken his place. I would guess that this set of circumstances led to the earlier illness in which Chris lost contact with reality and was hospitalized.

In view of these circumstances, he must have had considerable strength to pull himself together and get out of the hospital, and it is not surprising that anything which reminds him of the relationship with his father still disturbs him. The father produced a daughter, and at the same age Chris produces a daughter; the parallel situation may have set off a depression.

We don't know how he was diagnosed in the mental hospital after his father's death. He could have had a depressive type of illness or he could have been schizophrenic. His joining a different church so he can speak up about religious matters without feeling embarrassed makes me wonder how strange his ideas are. Bizarre and peculiar thinking is one of the symptoms of schizophrenia, and it may persist in an attenuated form after the acute illness is over.

CLERGYMAN 1: Perhaps he is working out part of his problem by speaking up in opposition to the church's customary position.

DR. ALDRICH: Yes, he could be funneling his aggression into the church situation. Perhaps this could explain why he irritates Mr. Cook. As a representative of the church, Mr. Cook offers a convenient target for working out Chris's problems. In discussing Mr. Armstrong's case [Chapter Two], we mentioned that the clergyman, as symbol of the powerful deity and as a father figure, gets more than his share of this type of displacement.

MR. COOK: Chris doesn't express open hostility toward me.

DR. ALDRICH: No, but you seem to sense it; I got the feeling, as you told us about him, that you don't like him very well.

MR. COOK: I thought we were going to analyze *him!*

DR. ALDRICH: I don't think you can really understand a person without looking at your own response to him. You can't help being irritated when you're being used as a target for anger that you didn't cause, and it's important not to try to maintain the fantasy that you're completely objective and that you love everybody equally. When I see a patient, I need to recognize the reaction that he stirs up in me, simply so that I can be more objective. If I insist that I am completely neutral and that everybody affects me in the same way, I am just fooling myself.

MR. COOK: There is another element that may be contributing to Chris's guilt. His father committed suicide during the day, and when they sent to the school to bring Chris home, they discovered that he was playing hooky.

DR. ALDRICH: Perhaps he was playing hooky to act out his rebellion against his father. Although it added to his guilt, playing hooky can also be perceived as a sign of strength. I am not suggesting that playing hooky is a good idea, but at least he was able to express his rebellion in some way; he was not so frightened by it that he had to hide it completely. His playing hooky may thus give us a clue to some of the strengths that have made him able to tolerate all these blows without folding up. He has troubles but he has something to work with. Perhaps his mother gave him the strength to adapt to this serious tragedy.

The family of a suicide needs a lot of help, and the adolescent child perhaps needs more help than anyone else with his feelings of guilt and responsibility. Be careful not to reassure him too quickly, however, because you may not be reassuring him about the right thing. Your impulse and mine—everybody's natural impulse—is to comfort the bereaved, but comforting doesn't always get to the point. Everybody else is comforting them. They need a chance to talk, first to express their grief and their guilt, and after that, to communicate their anger or ambivalent feelings if they are able. Even if anger is only a small part

of their feelings, it is the part that will cause trouble later on.
The adolescent needs a chance to talk out his surface feelings in
privacy and in an empathic atmosphere until he can get to the
feelings that really hurt. You have to be patient—you can't
force him to talk—but if he has a relationship with you that permits him to come to the point on his own terms, it will pay off.

In Chris's case, I think he is telling you in a somewhat veiled
fashion that he is considering suicide and that he wants help
with his depression. He still can't communicate directly; he's
speaking in an obscure and latent language. It is frightening
to hear somebody start talking about suicide; right away you
think you should get him to a psychiatrist. If you are too precipitate in referring him, however, you risk making him feel
that you don't accept him and that you want to get rid of him.
In a way, you do want to get rid of him for altruistic reasons,
but he may not so interpret it. On the other hand, if you don't
get him to a psychiatrist, you are saddled with a serious responsibility. You will feel very badly if he does commit suicide, and
you hadn't sent him to a psychiatrist. His request for an interview with you, however, is a sign that he is looking for another
way of solving his problems. If all he wanted was suicide, he'd
go ahead and do it. Ordinarily, therefore, you have time to discuss his problems with him and you do not have to make an immediate referral.

CLERGYMAN 4: Chris has made it more complicated by putting
it in a religious context.

DR. ALDRICH: Yes, he says he is only talking philosophy. The
trouble is that the more you know, the more it worries you. If
you could just take his philosophical talk at face value, you
wouldn't be so concerned, but you know he is talking about
himself.

CHAPLAIN NIGHSWONGER: When the person who talks about
suicide couches it in religious language, I think that we pastors

often move too quickly into religious interpretations; we sometimes try to avoid accepting the psychological message.

DR. ALDRICH: I think that one of the reasons you do so is that you're more comfortable in the religious context. It's the same way with the doctor; he's more comfortable talking about pills and physical troubles, so he diverts the conversation away from what's really troubling the patient. In either situation, the minister or the doctor stays where he's comfortable, and the poor patient or parishioner is kept from talking about the real problem.

CHAPLAIN NIGHSWONGER: We shouldn't altogether ignore the religious aspect; if this man is to develop a fulfilling religious life, he must in some way work out the role God plays in his life—as a judge, or as a creative part of human experience. This aspect, however, can wait until he's worked out his delayed grief. He has to express his grief before he can try to make meaning out of life. We have to be careful not to get too preoccupied with the religious side, just because we feel easier with it, or because we think we're obligated to do so.

DR. ALDRICH: Yes, I think I would cut off Chris's philosophical discussion; I don't think that it's unimportant, but first things come first. First he needs the feeling that you, as the representative of the church, understand his ambivalence and accept him with it.

CLERGYMAN 6: Is it proper to ask him straight out, "Are you talking about your father's suicide or are you thinking about yourself?"

DR. ALDRICH: I think you should not back away from that question, but it may need some preamble. It may be premature to come right out with, "Are you thinking of your own suicide?" So far he has been quite obscure, but I would ask him to tell me more about it. He is asking you what his father's suicide means; I'd try to find out what it means to him. You may get confirmation of your hunch that he is protecting himself by sublimating it all in philosophy. This response would reassure you that he is not acutely suicidal, and that although he is talking about himself, he is doing so in rather detached terms. Later you may find that the question comes up more naturally. I think it is an important question to work toward, but it should not be sprung on him right away.

Perhaps we should rehearse it. I'll be Mr. Cook, and Mr. Cook can be Chris.

SIMULATED INTERVIEW

"CHRIS": You know, I've been doing a lot of thinking about my religious commitment and I've needed help along this line for a long time. I've never talked to you much about my dad. He was really a very religious man and a very good man; just recently I've come to some conclusions that have helped me understand his suicide. Everybody thinks that a person who has committed suicide has committed an unpardonable sin. I was thinking, though, about that passage of Scripture that says if your eye offends you, you should pluck it out. In thinking about my father, and knowing how conscientious he was and how careful to do the right thing, I can easily see how in a moment of discouragement he could think that this verse was intended to apply to him. He undoubtedly blamed himself for many things in the family, so probably his suicide was not sinful so much as it was an effort to do the right thing.

"MR. COOK": He blamed himself for what kinds of things in the family?

"CHRIS": He probably felt responsible for the financial difficulties we had, and the strains on my mother, and the problems of the children, and all that kind of thing.

"MR. COOK": He held himself completely responsible for all these problems?

"CHRIS": I think so. He thought of himself as a failure and felt that the family would be better off without him.

"MR. COOK": You were how old when he died?

"CHRIS": I was fifteen.

"MR. COOK": Can you tell me something about your feelings during the period right after his death?

"CHRIS": Well, I felt very bad.

"MR. COOK": Yes, I can well imagine.

"CHRIS": The very day that he died, they couldn't find me for several hours. They sent to school for me, but I was playing hooky; so I didn't find out about it until I finally wandered home after school. They had found out that I hadn't gone to school, so I had added to the trouble.

"MR. COOK": That must have made you feel even worse.

"CHRIS": Yes, it sure did.

"MR. COOK": Then after that—what was going on when you did get home and found out that this tragedy had occurred?

"CHRIS": Well, everyone was upset about my father; and of course, they were upset about me too, and wondered what I had done, where I was, and so forth.

"MR. COOK": What happened to you for playing hooky?

"CHRIS": Nothing.

"Mr. Cook": You got away with it because of the situation?

"Chris": Yes, they were feeling too badly about my father.

"Mr. Cook": I can see why they might have ignored it, but how did it make you feel?

"Chris": Well, I certainly felt worse that it had happened on that day. If it had been any other day, I would have felt bad, but this made me feel much worse.

"Mr. Cook": The fact that you got away with it made you feel worse. If they found you had been playing hooky on an ordinary day, you would have been punished, but in this case the only consequences were within yourself.

"Chris": Yes, except that I punished myself.

"Mr. Cook": How did you punish yourself?

"Chris": Well, I haven't forgotten how I felt; I still remember.

"Mr. Cook": I wonder if you are still punishing yourself?

(End of simulated interview)

Dr. Aldrich: You see, I'm not talking about his punishing himself for his death wish or anything like that. Playing hooky is not too bad to recognize and to talk about. At the same time, we're both indirectly talking about the lack of punishment for his own bad feelings about his father. We don't have to speak about them directly; it would confuse and antagonize him if I said, "Part of you really wanted your father gone so that you could take his place," and furthermore he wouldn't believe me.

From talking about feeling badly when he played hooky,

and not having been punished for it, we can move gradually toward the feelings he still has about his father's death. I might say, "There are probably times when you feel particularly badly about your father's death," and I would expect him to say, "Yes, when something reminds me of him." It may be the anniversary of his death, it may be when he sees a baby girl, or when he goes to church, it may be something quite irrelevant—whatever he associates with his father. Perhaps he has transferred some of his feelings to Mr. Cook, and that is one of his reasons for going off to another church.

By this time you have established a relationship in which you're not talking about philosophy, but about his feelings of grief about his father. As he talks about his feelings, as he tells you how badly he feels and how many things stir up these feelings, I think then it is appropriate to say, "I wonder if sometimes you've felt the way your father did," bringing in his concern that he is failing his family and wondering if he, too, thinks his family would be better off without him.

If you lead up to it that way, it doesn't appear to be such a frontal assault as it would be if you started in by saying, "Are you thinking about suicide yourself?" In this more gentle but definite approach, he perceives you as understanding the basis for his suicidal thoughts, and I believe he would acknowledge them if he had them. Then I would ask, "What keeps you from it?" I would expect him to start giving reasons why it would be unfair to the family, such as that they would be left without support; "After all, I do work at two jobs," he might say. At this point I could say, "I wonder if you felt that what your father did was also unfair?" In this way I could try, without probing, to sanction indirectly some of the negative feelings he has had about his father—his anger that his father committed suicide and left his mother and him. I think that tacitly recognizing and accepting his anger in this area can be more helpful to his depression than anything else you can do.

A person doesn't commit suicide because someone asks him

about it; if you ask, "Have you thought of suicide?" in the proper context, he doesn't say, "No, I haven't, but it's a good idea," and then go out and slit his throat. If anything, it's the other way around. If he can share his feelings about his father's suicide with you, and if, instead of reinforcing his guilt by saying, "If you kill yourself, look what you'll do to your family," you indicate your appreciation of his feelings after his father's death—his grief that his father was gone and his concern about the consequences to the family—you will make your point. As you accept his ambivalence, and as he begins to feel that somebody in authority can understand the kind of mixed feelings he has had all these years, he will become a little less depressed.

CLERGYMAN 6: How can you structure the situation so that he will come back and begin to share some of this with you? I've found that some people like Chris will come once or twice, but to get them to sit still long enough really to work it out is difficult.

CHAPLAIN NIGHSWONGER: We often get frightened or aggravated, or both, with someone who talks about suicide, particularly with someone who doesn't go to our church or whom we find irritating. Consequently we may not make it clear that we want to see him again—we don't try to arrange another definite appointment. I think in some way we ought to communicate our expectations of a continuing relationship with him before we close the session.

DR. ALDRICH: Your feeling that you don't want to leave loose ends can also keep him from returning. It's natural to try to tie the whole thing up into a package at the end so that he'll feel better when he leaves, but this procedure may be interpreted by the parishioner as meaning that you want to get rid of him. He's very sensitive to rejection at this point. If you give him a formula to let him know what he should do and how he should feel, and then you tell him to come back, he may feel that he can only come back when he has accomplished all you've prescribed. Since he is not likely to be able to do it all, he may feel ashamed to come back, and in that way rejected.

You don't have to finish everything or answer every question in each session. Psychiatrists use an artificial number of minutes, traditionally fifty, to provide a definite stopping place. If you have no limit at which you say, "Well, time is up, but I'll see you next week," you tend to go on indefinitely. You can't finish the job in one session, and if you try, you're only going to get exhausted. He is too, and he also needs a period of time to work with what he's found out about himself. So when you say to Chris: "It was hard for you really to resent your father, whom you loved and who was gone. That must have been a difficult dilemma for you," you don't have to give him an answer. He has something to work on, and you can say: "I can see that this is pretty tough, and I think we ought to talk more about it. Can you come in and see me next week?"

CLERGYMAN 5: What about saying to him, "God has forgiven your father, and he'll forgive you."

DR. ALDRICH: That may be true, but I don't think he's ready to hear it yet. He might take it as evidence that you wanted to wrap it up and get rid of him. He may have more to talk about, and may fear that the forgiveness wouldn't extend to whatever else he has on his conscience; or it could make him feel more guilty because he can't yet accept God's forgiveness. Forgiveness acts somewhat like sympathy in a depression—if Chris feels unworthy of forgiveness, his depression may increase. Instead, you can let him know that it is not all going to be solved in one day, but that you are interested in helping him.

If he asks whether he should see a psychiatrist or a social worker, my answer would depend on the depth of his depression. In Chris's case, I'd say: "I don't know yet. I think we ought to talk a little more before we decide." His depression seems to have been going on for quite a while, and I do not see his present state as an emergency. Furthermore, although he's had psychiatric treatment in the past, he may feel ashamed of it, since he did not come right out and tell you about it.

Of course, I cannot be sure that he's not suicidal. I doubt it, but there is always a chance, and this is a tough spot to leave you in. You should ask him whether he has sleep problems. If he wakes up every morning feeling that his world is coming to an end and that there is no point in going on, you're going to have to make an immediate referral. From what we've heard, however, it doesn't sound as if he's going to try suicide tomorrow or the next day; he is being very indirect in his suicidal signals, and I would not want to refer him too abruptly. He's had a hard enough time relating to you, and so far he is doing so in symbolic rather than direct terms; if you immediately pick up the hidden content and send him off to the psychiatrist, he will see it as more rejection. On the other hand, after another interview or two, he probably will be talking much more freely and directly. Then you might ask, "Have you thought of seeking professional help from a psychiatrist or a social agency?" He might say, "The psychiatrists at the hospital were too busy," or "The social agency worker is on my wife's side, and I'd rather stay with you." At some time you must decide whether you feel you can and want to carry the burden he represents; it is a burden to take the responsibility for a man like this and always to be wondering if his wife will call up and say that he doesn't exist anymore, because he has done what his father did. On the other hand, if you make a referral whenever there is any suspicion of suicide, it will be difficult to deal with troubled people at all. Depression, either overt or disguised, exists in many and perhaps in most of the people whom you see, and you can't send them all off to the psychiatrist.

When you feel it is necessary, however, I think you should be frank; you can say: "You know, I would like to continue to work with you, but I cannot be sure enough about your diagnosis unless I ask a psychiatrist to see you and to give me his opinion about continuing these conversations. I don't think it's fair to you or to me unless we work it out on that basis." If he says he doesn't want to, you can reply firmly, "I know you don't want to, but I believe it is necessary," and he will probably agree. If he doesn't, and says, "Well, I'd rather quit the whole thing," you can say: "I don't think that's the answer. The answer is for you to go and see the psychiatrist, and then he will talk with me, and we'll figure out where to go from there. I'm not abandoning you, but I am insisting that I must get the kind of help I need." You must be firm and unequivocal if you have made up your mind that more help is required.

As you get more information about Chris, you may decide not to refer him. In that case, I think it would be best to see him alone, without his wife. When the major problem on which you are working antedates the marital relationship, it can confuse the issue to bring the other person into it. Chris's most significant problem dates back to a time before the wife came on the stage in this particular drama, so I think you're going to have to concentrate on him.

He needs to know that what he tells you is confidential. Although his wife is emotionally upset, I think you may have to stall for a while before working with her. When you decide to work with the marital problem, which she wants to work on, you can work with both of them.

CLERGYMAN 6: How did you categorize Chris in terms of the four types of depression that you outlined [Chapter One]?

DR. ALDRICH: I think that he suffers from the first type: prolonged unresolved grief reactive to guilt and ambivalence about the death of his father. We still don't have enough information about that period of his life, but you are likely to get more as you help him express his feelings about it. He might say, "You know, I had to go to a hospital after he died," and you could reply, "I knew that you did, but I don't know the details." At this point he might tell you how badly he felt about what happened.

On the other hand, he might say, "I don't want to stir all this up." You might go along with him at this point, if you thought it was safe, but I think it would be better to say, "I can see how it would be disturbing to stir it up; but I had a feeling that when you were telling me about the religious significance in his death, it was already stirred up."

Simply by taking the step of going to someone for help, or even just making an appointment, a person is often somewhat reassured. He shifts some of the burden onto the helping person, and therefore he no longer has the same pressure to talk about it. A parishioner may call you to say, "I am terribly anxious about my sex life (or my angry feelings) and I've got to see you." So you see him, and he says, "I don't want to talk about my sex life (or my angry feelings)." "But isn't that what you came in for?" "Yes, but it would upset me to talk about them." The reassurance of the helping relationship's existence is enough to support his capacity to repress, and that makes him feel better.

The reassurance may not take effect until after the first interview. He may tell you a great deal about his disturbed feelings in the first session, but when he returns, all the feelings seem to have disappeared. Establishing a relationship in itself may have been sufficiently helpful so that the specific nature of the trouble gets covered up.

When, as in Chris's case, the original trouble is something as dangerous as a suicide threat, it is especially important, first, to decide whether to uncover it again, and if so, when to initiate the process. Suicide threats, whether explicit or implicit, are frightening to therapists of any persuasion. If after careful evaluation, the clergyman can determine that the danger is not imminent, however, he may be able to support his parishioner past the danger point and carry out his customary counseling.

Chapter Five

MARITAL
BALANCE

The birth of Dan and Doris' first child disturbs the relatively precarious balance of their marital situation. As it becomes evident that the problem is mainly a lack of communication, the discussion focuses on how Mr. Davis can encourage more communication, and how he can help Doris by helping Dan recognize their problems. Some of the differences between the counseling roles of the clergyman and the psychiatrist are pointed out.

MR. DAVIS: Both Dan and Doris sang in the choir in my church, and Doris was secretary of the Ladies' Aid. He is an accountant, and she used to be a copywriter in an advertising agency. They were in their mid-thirties and had been married ten years without children.

One day at church, Dan said to me: "Guess what? Doris is pregnant." They were both elated and continued to be enthusiastic after she quit work. When their son arrived Doris seemed very excited, and I did not think anything was wrong when I saw her in the hospital and again, somewhat later, when the child was brought to church for baptism.

However, one night about two months after the baby's birth, Dan asked me to come to their home because Doris was very depressed. Her mother had been with them; when she left, it became clear that Doris was not feeling at all capable of taking care of the child. Part of the problem seemed to be caused by the fact that the child had a club foot which would require hospital treatment. Caring for the child seemed just too much for Doris, although she had always been extremely competent in anything she did.

We talked for some time. Dan's attitude was that the family was "finally complete," with the clear implication that the marriage had never been complete before. It seemed to me that as she sensed his response, Doris began to feel that she had been a failure for all the previous years, and that Dan's whole concern was for the baby.

She seemed overwhelmed, and I reinforced their doctor's suggestion of a visit to a psychiatrist. Dan hadn't liked the idea of a referral, chiefly because he didn't want anybody to know that there were any difficulties in the family. They went to the psychiatrist, however, and Doris entered the hospital for psychiatric treatment.

Shortly thereafter they left the neighborhood to stay with her parents. Only recently I discovered that Doris has been in the hospital a second time. I had not heard from them until a few weeks ago when Dan called me and said: "Well, we are back at home, now. Doris is still upset and can't seem to cope with the baby. Can you find somebody to help her?" I immediately called a nurse who belongs to the church and who offered to help, but the day before she was to start, Dan called her to say that they were going back to stay with Doris' parents.

I was upset when I heard about this, because I felt that moving to the parents' might be just temporizing. I think I failed somewhere along the line, but I don't know where. Perhaps I should have continued to work with them, even though I don't know if I would have accomplished much. Earlier I called the psychiatrist and asked him to call back, but he didn't. I didn't follow through after Doris went into psychiatric care, and I didn't follow through to see if I could reach them at their home. I think I could at least have given Dan some reassurance; he seemed afraid to face his neighbors, afraid to face his community, and his church. I don't know—maybe I didn't recognize what he needed.

DR. ALDRICH: Maybe you are being too hard on yourself. I am not sure that Dan could have accepted help any earlier. In fact, it may have been your lack of pressure on him that enabled him to ask you for help in finding a nurse; if you had insisted while he was denying his need for help, he might have built up his denial even more strongly. As I listened to you, I had the feeling that maybe in the long run you were better off not taking action. But it is hard to stand by and see things getting worse.

MR. DAVIS: I knew that I could do nothing for Doris because she was a psychiatrist's patient, but I felt a responsibility toward Dan. Maybe I could have done something for him.

CHAPLAIN NIGHSWONGER: Are you saying that sometimes we back off from a person while he is in the midst of this kind of crisis? Even if we are not formally counseling him, we should not break off communication just because we don't know how to relate to him. We pastors often run away from problems with a psychiatric overtone. I'm not saying that is what Mr. Davis did, but I thought Dr. Aldrich might have been making it a little too easy on him by justifying or at least supporting his reasons for not doing more in the situation.

DR. ALDRICH: Maybe so, but how would you manage it? At what point did he have a chance to intervene? It seems to me that Dan kept him at arm's length. How do you go about getting Dan involved until he is ready?

CHAPLAIN NIGHSWONGER: Well, it seems to me that the pastor has many avenues of relationship to both Doris and Dan. Weren't they both choir members and involved in many church activities? With the baby, their pattern of relationship to the church changed, but that did not mean that the pastor's frequent contacts had to be completely cut off. If these contacts are maintained, the opportunity of relating to Dan will come, not through coercion but through responding to him with support which then might very well open up the chance to help.

DR. ALDRICH: If Dan and Doris had stayed home instead of shuttling back and forth to her parents' home, the pastor would have had a better chance to help Dan.

CLERGYMAN 3: It seems to me that the problem is much deeper. I imagine that it existed before the child was born, even before Doris' pregnancy. Dan didn't want anybody to know about his family troubles; he had built a wall around himself so that he could not be approached. As the problem got worse, the wall became higher until he was so defensive that the pastor could not reach him at all—he simply ran away. To criticize the pastor because he hasn't succeeded in reaching this man seems unreasonable—he was destined to failure before he began.

DR. ALDRICH: Dan has made it hard for anyone to help him. However, when he asks about the nurse, he is looking for help from the pastor. At this point, the pastor may have more chance than the psychiatrist to help him.

CLERGYMAN 6: I am a little confused. Are you suggesting that Dan is a sick person as well as Doris?

MR. DAVIS: I think he was the sick one to begin with. He felt ashamed that his marriage wasn't completed with a child and he was making his wife feel responsible.

CLERGYMAN 6: Isn't it natural for a man who has been married ten years without children to say, "Hurrah! Finally I've got a son"? His only problem is his wife.

CLERGYMAN 3: Many women become depressed after the birth of a child. It's a normal reaction that passes with time. In this case, Dan was so anxious to be a complete person by having a child that he upset his wife. If he could have taken a different attitude, he could have supported her and nothing serious would have happened.

CHAPLAIN NIGHSWONGER: When two persons have been married so long, their lives become so interrelated that it is impossible to say which one is sick; we can't help one without helping the other.

DR. ALDRICH: I think you're right. Any situation of this kind probably should be looked at from the point of view of the *family* rather than that of the individual. You do not have to pin a psychiatric label on Dan, but he is involved in the problem.

CLERGYMAN 2: I imagine that the wife is intellectually and socially more competent than the husband. I run into this situation quite often. It works out all right until a crisis arises. Then the wife has to play her own role and bolster him up at the same time. If it's too much for her and she gets depressed, and if he has been relying on her (consciously or unconsciously), they both fall apart because there is no mutual support. When Doris gets depressed and needs Dan, I wonder if he has anything to contribute? Has he felt inferior all along and has he bolstered his own ego by acting aggressively? Who wears the pants in this family?

MR. DAVIS: I think Dan is sure he does, but I don't know them as well as I should. Dan has a responsible job; on the other hand, Doris' salary has always been adequate and has made her somewhat self-sufficient.

CLERGYMAN 6: Why didn't they have any children before?

MR. DAVIS: I think they started out by purposely postponing children.

DR. ALDRICH: A lot of families start with the idea that they will not have children until they are in better shape financially. But, as time goes on, they keep postponing it. After ten years, Dan and Doris had established patterns of interaction and roles within the marriage that apparently were reasonably satisfying, and everything was going pretty well. Do we know whether this was a planned or an unplanned pregnancy?

MR. DAVIS: I am sure it was unplanned. Although they said they had always wanted a baby, this one wasn't planned.

DR. ALDRICH: I think that Doris' feelings about her pregnancy are important. How does a woman feel about being pregnant? Usually she seems delighted, but that isn't always the whole story, particularly in a first pregnancy. She also resents it, although she may not be able to acknowledge her resentment even to herself. There are few women who are 100 percent enthusiastic about being pregnant for the first time. Their figures change and they wonder whether their husbands will be as attracted to them as before. They are scared of the process of birth; they are concerned about being cooped up in the house and about giving up things they enjoy. These ambivalent feelings may be even greater in a late pregnancy, when a wife's pattern of living is more set.

As in grief, the psychological consequences depend not so much on the quantity of ambivalence as on its acceptability. When a woman is pregnant for the tenth time, almost everybody commiserates with her; she may feel much more resentful about the tenth pregnancy than about the first, but she has much more support from the outside to help her feel that it is all right to wish that she weren't pregnant. But Doris is a woman who has always *wanted* a baby but never planned to have one, and now at the age of thirty-five discovers that she is pregnant. Everybody, including her husband, is elated. What does she do with her ambivalence? Who understands or helps her with the part of her that says, "Eight years ago this would have been fine, but now I'm not so sure"?

For a woman to wish she weren't pregnant has the same significance as for her to wish to have an abortion or a miscarriage. If Doris had had a miscarriage, I think she would have had an even more severe depression. It would seem to her that the wish for the child's death had actually caused the death. Earlier I discussed the child's feeling that if his wish is carried out by an agent beyond his control, he is responsible. I suspect that Doris wished at times that she weren't pregnant, and I also suspect that she interprets the club foot as God's punishment for her sinful wish.

I don't believe that she is conscious of these feelings; if she could recognize them, she would be able to understand them better in the light of reality, and accept the reassurance that a club foot could not result from hostility or ambivalence or any other feeling. But without knowing they exist, she cannot cope with them rationally, and they are so upsetting that she cannot acknowledge their existence.

So, although Dan isn't the patient, he could have counteracted some of the effects of his wife's ambivalence; it would have helped if he had been able to communicate to her that, as far as he was concerned, the pregnancy didn't have to be an unmixed blessing. Obstetricians, family doctors, pastors, and particularly husbands might help prevent many of these depressions if they would not imply that a pregnant woman has to feel elated, and that any other feeling but elation means that she is bad. Of course, you have to have an opening before you can communicate your acceptance of ambivalence, and I don't think Mr. Davis got the opening.

CLERGYMAN 5: Do you mean that if Dan had accepted her mixed feelings, and had told her that he accepted them, her depression might not have occurred?

DR. ALDRICH: I think it would have helped if Dan had said, at the time when she had to quit work: "It must be tough to give up a job that you've done so well at. You must really feel disappointed." She might have said: "Oh, no. It's great to be pregnant at last," but he has made his point; he has said that it is all right with him for her to have mixed feelings. Even though she disclaims her ambivalence, she gets his message. He doesn't have to insist; he can just let her know that as far as he is concerned, she doesn't have to feel that *everything* about it is wonderful.

CLERGYMAN 5: Wouldn't another woman, who knows what she is going through, be more helpful? Her mother, perhaps, or a friend?

DR. ALDRICH: Another woman has more knowledge of pregnancy, but someone of either sex can communicate an understanding of her ambivalence. In Doris' case, her mother may not be the best choice. In the second step of her development, when she was learning to control her aggressive impulses, she probably learned from her parents that it is bad to be hostile; this would make it hard for her to cope with her ambivalence.

MR. DAVIS: That makes sense to me; Doris never seems to express anger or hostility toward anyone.

DR. ALDRICH: I imagine that she could never permit herself to say, when she was vomiting or when she couldn't get into her girdle, "Oh, if only I weren't pregnant." That would mean to her that she wished the baby would die, which would in turn mean that she might cause the baby's death.

CLERGYMAN 6: Many mothers wish they weren't pregnant and many of them can't acknowledge hostility, but they don't all end up going to a psychiatrist. What is different about Doris?

Dr. ALDRICH: There are at least three ways in which Doris differs from the average mother, and there may be more that we don't know about. Probably none of these in itself is enough to cause her depression, but the combination makes the difference. First is the life pattern she established over the years. It is fairly easy for a girl of twenty-two, who has worked two or three years as a secretary to give up her job; it is much more difficult at thirty-five, after ten years in a job with major responsibility. The second reason concerns Dan; he supports only the positive side of her response to pregnancy and so adds to the pressures toward depression. The third point is the child's handicap, which seems to constitute retribution for her hostile feelings; in this case it falls not on her, but on her innocent child. If she had been able to look at her hostile feelings, she would have realized that this sequence didn't make sense, that she could feel as angry as she liked, and no one would be killed and no one's foot deformed as a result. But she buried these feelings at an age when she assumed that the thought caused the event, so that internally she now believes that anything which happens to the child is her fault. Women often attribute a child's mental retardation or congenital defect, or a miscarriage, to some kind of transgression. You have probably all heard a woman in this situation say, "I must have done something to deserve this."

CHAPLAIN NIGHSWONGER: Can you go so far as to say that people who can accept and express their ambivalence don't get depressed?

Dr. ALDRICH: I would not go quite that far, but I do think that a person's management of his ambivalence is the most important factor. Depression is much less likely to occur in people who have both the internal ability to accept ambivalence and external support in expressing it. On the other hand, Doris might have escaped without a serious depression if the child had been normal. Any one of the factors we have discussed might be crucial.

CLERGYMAN 8: Doris was hospitalized twice and apparently received some sort of therapy both times. Why wasn't she helped?

DR. ALDRICH: I don't know what it was about her case that led to her failure to respond. Ordinarily, this kind of patient can be helped, although when hostile feelings are repressed early in life, their expression is difficult to modify. If she could recognize her hostility at all, she should have been helped by psychotherapy. On the other hand, she may have been so seriously depressed that the psychiatrist felt he had to take more drastic measures, such as shock treatments.

CLERGYMAN 8: Do you think that organic or chemical changes might be causing the depression?

DR. ALDRICH: Her story suggests to me that psychological factors are chiefly responsible. However, I also expect that the doctor looked for organic factors. I assume that he found none or, if he found any, that they were in addition to, not instead of, the psychological factors.

CLERGYMAN 5: Some psychiatrists appear to pay no attention to the personality development approach to diagnosis; for them it is only shock or drug therapy.

DR. ALDRICH: Psychiatry is far from an exact science, and there are many valid ways of viewing the same patient. There are varying points of departure in psychiatry just as there are in your field. In general, drugs and shock treatment represent covering measures. They are used to try to strengthen the patient's defenses against recognizing his underlying conflicts rather than to attempt to understand him in terms of personality development. Psychotherapy takes such a lot of time, and psychiatrists are in such short supply compared to the number of patients needing treatment, that less time-consuming methods may be required to get the job done. Half the hospitalized patients in this country are psychiatric patients, and a lot fewer than half the doctors are psychiatrists. With thousands of patients in state hospitals, and a handful of doctors, the doctors do not have the time to sit down and listen to all their patients' problems.

The same discrepancy between supply and demand holds true in office practice. This discrepancy is one reason why professional people on the firing line in the community—general practitioners, clergymen, social workers—are treating some people for whom ideally, perhaps, psychiatric care is indicated. But we do not have and never will have enough psychiatrists with enough time to give the most appropriate kind of care to everyone who could use it. Doris, therefore, may have received less psychiatric attention than she should have received, or she may not have responded well to treatment. Even in the best hands psychiatric treatment is often unpredictable and unsuccessful.

Ideally a patient's spouse receives attention, often from a psychiatric social worker, while the patient is hospitalized. But this type of care is also in short supply, and we don't know whether Dan received help while his wife was under psychiatric care.

Assuming that he did not, what is transpiring when he asks Mr. Davis about the nurse? He isn't saying directly, "I need help for myself," when he says "I need a nurse"; but people often conceal what they really want by asking for something else. Mr. Davis sensed that Dan wanted more than a nurse. If he goes no farther than getting the nurse for him, he may be missing a hidden message that is beneath the obvious message.

What could Dan want to say? He may want to say that he

feels as responsible as Doris does for the child's deformity. He may want to say that his elation about her pregnancy was his way of covering up for negative feelings. He may have thought, "I need a child to prove that I am a man, but I wish I didn't have to do it in a way that upsets my wife."

We still don't know the nature of his feelings about the child. He may need the child so much for his own reasons that he resents the child's relationship to its mother. He may have been unconsciously competing with his wife for the child even before the child was born. Why else did *he* give up the choir? Doris had to give it up, since she was going to have to feed and care for the baby, but why did he give it up as well? To be "complete," does he have to be both mother and father? Or does the choir have some special significance for him? If you are ashamed, you stay away from a place that reminds you of your shame. If Dan feels ashamed of the child's deformity, he may want to stay away from the place where he had talked so much about Doris' pregnancy.

All these ideas so far are only speculations. How would Mr. Davis find out if any of them are valid? Asking Dan might not give him the answer—Dan wouldn't be likely to be aware of feelings such as envy of his wife's maternal role. These are unconscious, but they can be inferred from other data. To form a tentative hypothesis about Dan, Mr. Davis would have to know a lot more about him: where he was in his family, what his parents were like, what kind of childhood he had.

In a way, however, the nature or even the existence of a hidden message isn't yet the pastor's business. Dan hasn't come to the point of really letting his hair down. First, he needs an opportunity and some encouragement to acknowledge that events after the child's birth have been perplexing and disappointing, perhaps almost overwhelming. If the pastor accepts these feelings, Dan may be able to say that he was worried about the pregnancy from the beginning. He then might reveal his feelings about not having had a child earlier in the mar-

riage and talk about some of the factors in his own life that
have worried him; out of this may come some recognition that
he and his wife share more problems than either has been able
to acknowledge. I think that counseling Dan may indirectly
help Doris, just as in some situations you may be able to help
a child through talking with the parent.

CLERGYMAN 1: You mentioned that finding out about Dan's
past history was not yet the pastor's business. When Dan does
come to the point of recognizing that he has a problem and
that he wants some help with it, how does the pastor get the
history? We have been conditioned by the nondirective
(Rogerian) approach not to probe and not to ask questions
that might relate to earlier developmental problems, and yet
you imply that we shouldn't let the discussion be entirely
unstructured.

CHAPLAIN NIGHSWONGER: I think that ministers aren't sure how
appropriate it is for them to focus an interview, to ask questions
that will direct the counselee into areas of his life or feelings
that he has not volunteered. We've been told that when we do
so, we are being too authoritarian and we are not allowing the
counselee to grow and work through his problems for himself.
We get the idea that whenever we ask a question or direct the
focus, we're probing. Maybe it would be helpful to clarify the
difference between probing and simply finding out more information.

DR. ALDRICH: I think that anything that the counselee is aware
of and is willing to communicate to the pastor, with some encouragement, comes under the heading of information that is
appropriate for the pastor to obtain. Probing to me means
seeking information by putting the counselee under duress,
making him feel obligated to reveal what he wants to conceal.
   For example, at an appropriate time in my history taking, I

may ask a patient, "Do you recall any time when you've been particularly troubled about masturbation?" I try to choose my words and to use a tone of voice which will convey to him that he is free to tell me or not to tell me. I wait to ask him until he has reason to believe that my interest in this subject is related to my interest in helping him and that my emphasis is on whether he has been troubled rather than on how he has acted, but he still is free to avoid the issue.

So far, I am finding information. If he denies any trouble, however, and I say: "Come on, now, you know that the Kinsey report found that everybody masturbates. How can you expect me to help you if you don't tell me what's bothering you?" I am probing. It's a matter of degree, but my rule of thumb is that you are not probing if the counselee feels really free to withhold information.

CLERGYMAN 1: This distinction is helpful. However, I would like to know whether there is a formula that we can use to obtain historical material for our counseling.

DR. ALDRICH: Unfortunately, there is no formula that applies to every case, and I'm not suggesting that you take a formal history on your counselees. Perhaps we might illustrate the procedure I'm talking about. Mr. Davis, you know Dan fairly well. Can you act his role, while I act yours? How did Dan approach you? I'll try to respond as I think you might under these circumstances.

SIMULATED INTERVIEW

"DAN": Well, as you know, we've had some problems. And right now, well, it's pretty rough. We thought it would be over with by now. But at the moment I guess I'll have to have some help. You said once before that if there were any ways in which we could use help, I should contact you, and that is what I am coming for. I need somebody to help Doris now, when I am at work. Somebody who can be in during the day. Is there anybody like that in the parish?

"Mr. Davis": I don't know, Dan, I think we might be able to help you out with somebody like that, but first could you tell me a little more about how Doris is doing now?

"Dan": Well, Doris still says she doesn't know if she can take care of the child, and she throws up her hands and goes into her room. She says, "I just can't do it."

"Mr. Davis": What do you think about that?

"Dan": Well, I think she could if once she'd get over this fatigue. She's been all worn out. Her nervous breakdown took something out of her physically. If someone were there to help her so she would gain confidence while she recovers her strength, she'd be all right.

"Mr. Davis": How do you respond to her when she says that she just can't do it?

"Dan": Oh, I just tell her she really can, and she needs some faith in God. She could do it.

"Mr. Davis": And then what happens? Does this . . .

"Dan": Well, once in a while I think that maybe she's going to come along and I can give her some support, but sometimes she just throws up her hands and says she can't.

"Mr. Davis": It's kind of hard for her to accept your reassurance when things have been so tough?

"Dan": Well, we were doing fine and this is just momentary, but right now we do need some help. I thought it would be over with by now, but it is still . . .

"Mr. Davis": It has been discouraging to you too? Tell me . . .
I would like to know a little more about the beginning, when
Doris first began to have some doubts about her ability to cope
with the baby.

"Dan": Well, you know how she was. She had always been so
busy at work, and I helped her at home; and when she left
work, I think she had more time on her hands and she just
began to worry, particularly the last month or two. She had
been feeling well up until then.

"Mr. Davis": Until she changed the whole situation by leaving
the job. And you kept encouraging her that she could do it all
right?

"Dan": Oh, yes. Sure. God gave us a baby. We are capable of
taking care of it.

"Mr. Davis": When did you first realize that the baby was
handicapped?

"Dan": Well, we were told a little bit about it right after the
birth, or I guess it was a little later, I don't recall. But they told
us that it would be taken care of.

"Mr. Davis": How did you feel when you first heard about it?

"Dan": Well, you know there are problems you have to face.
You just take it.

"Mr. Davis": I wonder if you had any idea in your mind as to
how you could account for it?

"Dan": No. It is just one of those matters of luck, I guess. It
just happens. Luck.

(End of simulated interview)

DR. ALDRICH: My goal at this point would be to try to see if I couldn't help Dan question this explanation a little. You know, he said God gave the baby. I might go so far as to say that God also gave the club foot. This is pushing Dan a bit, but remember, he's not the one who has collapsed and so he can take the pushing better than she can. If I then said, "Did Doris have any idea about how the baby came to be deformed?" what would he say? I am not disguising the facts; I am saying "deformed" because that's what it is.

MR. DAVIS: I don't know what he would have said.

DR. ALDRICH: Well, take a guess.

MR. DAVIS: I think that he probably would have indicated that Doris was disturbed by it, but I don't know.

DR. ALDRICH: What I expect will come out is what you are saying indirectly: there hasn't been much *communication* about it. And that, you see, is where I am heading. He is going to say, though not directly, "I don't *know* how Doris feels about it." And then I'm going to say something to the effect that, "I know this has been pretty upsetting to both of you, and yet I get the feeling that, in some way, it has been difficult for you to talk with each other about it." I think he can acknowledge that there hasn't been much communication.

If so, I will ask Dan how he accounts for the lack of communication. Dan then may say, "Well, we've always shared all kinds of things, except that there are some areas that seem a little more difficult to share." From this beginning, I am going to lead him to speculate about her feeling of disappointment about the baby, and the possibility that she somehow might have felt responsible for the deformity. As he tries to imagine her feeling of disappointment, I think that some of his feelings will come out, including feelings that he has let her down. I would use our exploration of the possible bases for her depression to help him gradually recognize his own feelings. And then I would let him share his disappointment, frustration, and sadness with me; out of *that* I could help him feel more free to help her express her feelings—her inner, deeper, conscious, but still concealed feelings—so that they can work together with the negative as well as the positive.

If they can share their feelings, he won't have to reassure her all the time. Although he says reassurance sometimes helps, he may not recognize its real effect on her. If someone can't cope with a problem, and has tried and tried and tried and still can't make it, and I say, "Don't worry, you can do it," he feels either that I don't understand him or that he must be a terribly inadequate person because he can't do what I seem to think is so easy. Reassurance, therefore, can make a depressed person more depressed.

I wouldn't just tell Dan not to reassure his wife, because he would not see the reason for that; he has to work through to some understanding of his own about reassurance. I can lead him to the point where he can see and accept how terrible and how guilty she feels, and then I can help him to see that sharing similar feelings of his own perhaps can give her the moral strength, if you will, to go ahead and cope better.

In the interview that Mr. Davis and I simulated, I responded to comments that seemed relevant to my goal of involving him, and did not respond to comments that did not seem relevant. Although I cut him off about his request for a nurse to come in, I didn't overlook it. Before the interview was over, I would say, "You know, Dan, some of the things we have been discussing today make me feel that if we talked a little more about them it would help you to be even more helpful to your wife." I present it to him in a positive way. I don't say, "You *haven't* been helpful to your wife," but instead, "If we talk some more, you can be *more* helpful to your wife."

I'd then go on to say: "I'm sure that a nurse can be found, although bringing someone in from the outside may confirm

Doris' feeling that she can't do it. But let me check around a bit, and when you come in next week, we'll talk some more about it. Meanwhile, I'll see who's available." I am not going to accept his need for a nurse as the real problem until I know a little more, but I would find out who might be available in case, at the next visit, it seems a more appropriate solution than it did at first. Finally, if Dan does not see my point, but still has a great need to reassure Doris in order to reassure himself, I would consider seeing the two of them together, although this would depend on the status of her psychiatric care.

CLERGYMAN 7: Wouldn't it be better for the pastor to do it by dropping into the home for a call?

DR. ALDRICH: A call would be easier for them. But I wouldn't want to visit until Dan sees its purpose, and he might want to have another couple of talks with me before I dropped in and talked with both of them. I wouldn't do it under false pretenses; she should know why I'm there. My role with them would be to expedite their communication with each other about the difficult things in their lives, so that they won't each have to try to cover up for the other, and so that they can share more with each other.

CHAPLAIN NIGHSWONGER: I want some clarification about the role you are playing here. Are you responding as you perceive the minister might respond, or as you as a doctor would, or are you making any distinction?

DR. ALDRICH: I'm not making much distinction as far as the goal of my response and the technique of my intervention are concerned. Some of the circumstances are different, however.

CLERGYMAN 8: Yes, the fact that Dan and the pastor are on a first-name basis makes a difference. He's not pushing a complete stranger, he's pushing a person that he's known a long time.

DR. ALDRICH: That's an important distinction; the psychiatrist's role is sometimes easier because there are fewer complicating factors. For one thing, the psychiatrist is not very likely to encounter his patient in a social situation, when the patient might be embarrassed in recalling what he had revealed in treatment. But the pastor continues in his pastoral role as well as his counseling role.

CLERGYMAN 1: As long as you are in the pastor's role, this is a good time to ask you a couple of questions. What you said could well have been said by a family counselor or social worker or doctor. But suppose that Dan said: "Why in the world did this happen to us? This loving, merciful, great God of yours, why did he let this little baby suffer?" Of course, Dan doesn't sound like a person who might react in this way. But wouldn't this be an opportunity for the pastor to broaden the framework, to help him to talk about how angry he is at God and to reassure him that the loving God does not mean that God is someone he always has to have positive feelings about?

DR. ALDRICH: I am a little out of my depth. Is there a way of coping with this question without making him feel guilty about his anger at God? Because, you see, he may be using this as a test to find out if you really mean that it's all right for him to express hostility.

CHAPLAIN NIGHSWONGER: This kind of complaint happens more than you think. Somewhere our parishioners get the idea that if God is the God of perfect love, you cannot question him or blame him and you cannot feel anything but love for him. But the Bible clearly contradicts the notion that negative feelings toward God cannot be expressed. The psalmists frequently express man's anger at God, as in the first verse of the Twenty-second Psalm, which Christ himself used on the cross when he felt so alone in his agony: "My God, my God, why hast thou forsaken me?"

It seems to me that we pastors can do more than we often do to support and help the suffering person express feelings of anger about why a tragedy happened to him.

CLERGYMAN 2: Maybe it is putting you on the spot, but as a psychiatrist, what kind of response would you give if a patient said to you, "Why has God done this to me?"

DR. ALDRICH: In this situation I wouldn't feel that I had to come up with an answer. The psychiatrist's concern with a patient's religious attitudes is only to understand how his view of religion affects his feelings. I think it would be easier for me than for you simply to reflect the patient's feeling and say, "You feel deserted," or "You feel this must be a punishment," or something like that. You see, my collar is the other way around. Perhaps that is why patients don't ask me this question or, at least, they don't ask it expecting an answer. They may ask it of me as a rhetorical question, but I don't have as much of a problem in helping them see and express their anger because I'm not a representative of God.

CLERGYMAN 3: I'm not sure that people ask that question of ministers, except rhetorically, even in moments of extreme stress.

CLERGYMAN 5: It seems to me that we face two dangers in pastoral counseling. One is that we won't understand the sort of thing we are talking about here. The other is the danger of playing junior psychiatrist and forgetting that our real training is theological.

CLERGYMAN 2: But should we try to hang a cross on everything we do? Sometimes we push things into religious contexts when the real religious question is whether or not we care and whether or not we are involved in people's problems. This, to me, is a theological concern.

DR. ALDRICH: It is hard to avoid one of two extremes. At one extreme, you may forget that your real role is that of a clergyman. At the other extreme, you may fall back on the traditional exhortative role of the clergy, to the exclusion of the counseling role. It is the same way with the family doctor. His patient avoids a touchy subject by saying, "I've got a new pain." And if the family doctor is not comfortable in managing the emotional problem, he picks up his stethoscope and diverts the whole interaction into a traditional medical area. Both of them are relieved, but the problem isn't solved.

CHAPLAIN NIGHSWONGER: Just as the minister and the parishioner may join each other in directing the trend of the interaction to prayer or to the Bible.

DR. ALDRICH: Of course, there are times when it is essential to pick up the stethoscope or to pick up the Bible. But there are also times when both parties use diversionary tactics to avoid the kind of discomfort that you saw developing between Mr. Davis and me when I was playing his role and he was playing Dan's. I wasn't making "Dan" comfortable; I wasn't making him feel better. And neither of us felt as easy in this situation as we would have if I had simply said, "Dan, I know how tough it has been and I will find that nurse." If I had said that, he would have felt better, and I would have felt better, at least temporarily, but we would have avoided the basic issue.

CLERGYMAN 2: You were pushing him all right; how can you avoid pushing too hard, so that he freezes instead of opening up?

DR. ALDRICH: I usually try to avoid going too fast by making my questions tentative. If I say, "Do you *suppose* you *might* have had some misgivings about this child?" it's less threatening than saying flatly, "You had some misgivings about this child." If I say, "Do you suppose?" he can say, also tentatively, "No, I don't think so"; he has an escape hatch. I may go on to ask, "You are sure?" and he might say: "Yes, I am real sure. Aren't you?" Then I could say, "Well, you know there are some feelings that we are not aware of," and he might begin to question his assumption.

I don't think you hurt anybody if you make your approach tentative enough. You don't just shoot in the dark; you work out a possibility, you present it tentatively, and if he doesn't accept it, you accept his refusal. That doesn't mean you have thrown the idea away; you have put the bug in his ear, but you haven't forced the issue. On the other hand, if you make a blunt or disturbing interpretation like, "Really, behind all this, you wanted her to lose the baby," you can scare the daylights out of him. A good rule for interpretation is not to go beyond a reasonable hypothesis to which you think he might respond with, "You know, that's a possibility, I've wondered about that." If you can conceive of a patient or parishioner giving serious consideration to your interpretation, you're not likely to hurt him. But if, as you anticipate how he is likely to respond, you think he will be horrified or shocked, perhaps you should postpone it. I don't think very many people are hurt by inaccurate interpretations, but you may hurt the relationship by scaring him off.

So, although I have no easy formulas for solving marital problems, I think you will be able to help Dan in the ways we have discussed, and through him, to help Doris. It's sometimes frustrating not to have formulas; the only consolation is that formulas would make counseling less of a challenge, and less rewarding to the counselor.

Chapter Six

DELINQUENCY

Edward's case illustrates the relationship between delinquent behavior and problems of hostility and dependency. His failure to develop an effective conscience is tied to his relationship with his family and their expectations of him. The clergyman, by maintaining his own position as a counselor and not as an adjunct of the family or the law-enforcement agencies, can often help delinquents through working with the parents and through making clear his own positive expectations of the delinquent child.

MR. ELLIS: Edward, age twenty-one, is presently in jail awaiting trial for being involved with another man in a robbery and beating about three weeks ago. He claims he did not participate actively but he was present. His parents asked me to see him after he had written them from jail and told them that he had gone up to the altar at the church service and had prayed to God about all his troubles, and that he now feels better about all of them. He dropped out of high school to join the Marines and has had trouble adjusting to civilian life since his discharge. His father and mother are hard-working, conscientious people.

While Edward was in high school, he was active in the youth group of the church. His younger sister, who is nineteen, told me some things about Edward that neither he nor his parents had mentioned, for example, that during his adolescence he was frequently in minor scrapes and trouble. Outwardly, he and his father argued all the time, but, in her opinion, they were really "buddies." Every time he got in trouble, his dad would get him out of it in one way or another. She told me that he was drinking regularly before he ever went into the Marines. His parents, however, gloss over his adolescent troubles and blame his downfall on drinking in the Marines.

Soon after his discharge, Edward started going out with a divorced woman and staying out until 3 A.M. His mother told me that one of the first things he said to her when he came home from the Marines was: "Look, I am a man now. I don't want you telling me when I have to be home at night."

During the last year he has either quit or been fired from three jobs, and has been behind bars twice. He was employed by the company for which his father has worked all his life. Every time he quits a job or gets in trouble, his father still helps him out. He is now looking for a job, but his father's company has refused to give him another chance.

At his parents' request, I saw Edward in the hospital about six months ago. He ended up in the hospital with pneumonia because he had not followed his doctor's orders. When I came to see him, the nurses at first couldn't find him. When they finally found him, they were annoyed with him, telling him he had to stay in bed and asking me to persuade him to do so. He doesn't want to respect any restrictions.

I visited him at the city jail two weeks ago. He first told me that he had been to church and that he was really all right. I let him go on like that for a while, saying only that although I certainly couldn't approve of what he had done, and the church couldn't approve of it, I was there to try to help him. He responded to my offer of help by asking me to appear as a character witness at the trial. I guess he had been talking to an attorney.

I agreed to do so, because I thought that if I could show him that I was interested enough to be at the trial, I might develop enough of a relationship to help him. He has a somewhat distrustful attitude toward people in general, although it is not completely hostile. At the same time, I tried to get across the idea that I really didn't know that much about him.

Edward says now that he has been hanging around with the wrong kind of people and that he is going to have to change. He quit one job, against his parents' wishes, and sat all evening from 7 until 2 in the morning, waiting for some friends who were supposed to take him to a construction job in Texas. He was sure that they would come and was shaken when they never did. Most of the time, however, he acts completely sure of himself.

When I said that I would like to do anything I could to help him, he said, "Maybe you could tell some of the people around the church and around the town that I am really all right." I suppose this is something I could do—certainly I want to make it as easy for him as possible. But he doesn't seem to see me as the kind of helpful person that a psychiatrist would be. I don't know if he even thought of talking with a counselor, except as a way out of his trouble.

DR. ALDRICH: Is this a common kind of problem in your parishes?

CLERGYMAN 8: It is certainly common; I could name thirty families within a stone's throw of my church whose youngsters have been in and out of jails. But I don't see how this case belongs in a discussion of emotional disturbance. Are delinquency problems really the same as emotional problems?

CLERGYMAN 4: It seems to me that they represent a variety of emotional disturbance and they are so common that the pastor ought to be able to do a reasonably adequate job of rehabilitation with them.

CLERGYMAN 6: Yes, I can think of four or five in my own congregation and I have not felt very adequate in helping them through these situations.

CLERGYMAN 2: Do psychiatrists include delinquency in the category of emotional disturbance?

DR. ALDRICH: Most psychiatrists view delinquency that occurs in a generally law-abiding family and neighborhood as an emotional problem, just as they consider alcoholism an emotional problem. But for purposes of your counseling, I don't think you have to categorize people as either emotionally disturbed or emotionally healthy. In a way, the patient, or client, or parishioner makes the definition by the way he or his family or those about him look at his problem, directly or indirectly. Your role is determined by whether someone involved in the situation is seeking help, and by whether you can provide it or help him to find it.

In Edward's case, he seems to be indirectly seeking help with his emotional problems, although Mr. Ellis thinks he might be simply trying to get out of trouble.

CLERGYMAN 3: What was the relationship between Edward and his father in the years just before adolescence? Did his father give him any chance to demonstrate his ability to learn from his mistakes? After he returned from the Marines he talked a lot about being a man and not wanting interference, but if he lost his job or got in a scrape, his father always shielded him and so he never faced up to his problems.

I also wonder how well the father really knew his son. What kind of "buddies" were they? Did they go off on fishing trips together? Or was father so tied up with his job that he could only spare a few minutes at the end of the day? Perhaps the only way Edward could get attention when he was a teen-ager was by getting into trouble. The delinquent adolescent boys with whom I have worked did not have close relationships with their fathers.

DR. ALDRICH: That is a common thread in studies of delinquent adolescent boys.

CLERGYMAN 2: The idea of "buddies" came from the sister. Could she resent her older brother, who could always count on Dad to get him out of any scrape?

DR. ALDRICH: You wonder if rivalry between the sister and the brother distorts her picture of the relationship between father and son. There are many families in which the male has a higher value than the rest of the culture gives him. Do you think she feels that Edward was so favored?

CHAPLAIN NIGHSWONGER: Perhaps Edward has strong feelings of competition with his father? Does he feel inferior and could that account for his emphasis on being grown-up and wanting to assert himself?

MR. ELLIS: I'm not sure I can give you an accurate answer to any of these questions without more conversations with the family.

CLERGYMAN 1: But you agreed to be a character witness!

MR. ELLIS: That's right. I didn't want to, but he wanted me to, and I felt I had to do something. When I acted as a character witness on an earlier occasion, the attorney thanked me because he thought I got the boy off. On another occasion the boy was given probation, and then complained that I was too honest. I feel uncomfortable in these situations, because judges often seem to have a naïve notion about how much we are able to do. They give me more opportunity to speak out than they would give to a witness who wasn't a pastor. And sometimes they want to parole a boy to the pastor. I'm uneasy about that, because I feel that it might be more than I could handle.

DR. ALDRICH: The judge is relieved to find somebody in the community who is interested in the boy. So when he sees you in court, he says: "Fine. I will parole him in your custody. Next case." And he's all yours.

MR. ELLIS: And I know from experience that I am not so firm as I should be. Edward needs someone who is interested in him but, at the same time, someone who doesn't let him get away with anything. What do I do when the word gets back to me that he isn't getting home at night when he says he is?

DR. ALDRICH: Should you turn him in because he has violated parole? Should you tell the judge, "This kid stayed out till two o'clock when he was supposed to be in at midnight"?

CLERGYMAN 8: The "buddy" father would come down hard on the pastor. He would say: "Look, this was just an accident. They were out a little bit too late. They forgot the time. Haven't you ever been late when you were supposed to be in on time?" and so on.

CLERGYMAN 2: "Besides, I was pretty rowdy myself, when I was a kid."

CLERGYMAN 4: "And I outgrew it, so he will outgrow it. He needs to sow his wild oats."

DR. ALDRICH: You seem familiar with the father's reaction, which is really the most significant part of the problem. But what are the impulses or drives that are being expressed in Edward's behavior? Some of it is behavior that society prohibits: he robs and beats up a man. He also rebels against the family's way of life and he doesn't take care of his pneumonia. Most of the impulses that are expressed in these activities are aggressive impulses.

As I mentioned before, these impulses appear to be derived from the self-assertion of the second developmental stage and later reactivated in adolescence. In Edward's case, they are, for the most part, directed against authority, as if he were still involved in asserting his independence, even though he's old enough to have been in the Marines. During earlier developmental phases he hasn't developed the kind of controls of aggression that most people have. He hasn't incorporated controls into his adaptational system—instead, he still sees control as something superimposed on him by his family. He says, "I am now a man and not under your control," but he doesn't have controls of his own to take their place.

His rebellion against the doctor's orders and against the hospital nurses has elements of a rebellion against authority, but it also may reflect a residual problem in the first, or dependency, phase. To be ill and to need care may be so frightening that he can't let himself be cared for, so he behaves in a "pseudoindependent" manner. He seems to have to prove that he doesn't need to be taken care of by anybody, even when he is ill or hurt. A dependent situation stirs up his anxiety and makes him feel that he has to get out of bed. In a way such self-assertion appears to him to be the solution to the trap of dependency. He tries to avoid dependency by being aggressive and by challenging all authority, all people on whom he might be tempted to depend.

Many people have continuing problems with hostility and dependency. They don't all behave as Edward does, however. Most of them bottle up their anger and their anxiety about dependency, or take it out in harmless activities, or express it through neurotic symptoms. Edward differs in that he expresses his aggression directly.

So in addition to understanding the nature of the impulses he expresses, we need to know why his impulses are not kept from direct expression by the kind of barrier that people ordinarily develop within themselves. He knows the difference between right and wrong and he's aware when he has been bad. But awareness still doesn't protect him from bad behavior.

CLERGYMAN 1: He is aware that he is in trouble, but he wants Mr. Ellis to be a character witness to get him out of trouble. I'm not sure that he has any sense of responsibility for having gone against the laws of the church or the laws of society.

CLERGYMAN 7: It is the logical outcome if his father always got him out of jams and he suffered none of the consequences. There are parts of his conscience that just were not made airtight.

DR. ALDRICH: Your emphasis on his "buddy" father's condoning his behavior is right on target. Some years ago, it was assumed that behavior like Edward's was due to inborn criminal tendencies. Now most authorities put more emphasis on social or psychological causes. Social causes seem more significant in causing antisocial behavior in deprived families; psychological causes seem more significant in cases like Edward's.

One psychological theory developed from an experience of Drs. Johnson and Szurek of Chicago, who were concerned with behavior problems of children. The problem that provided the key to their theory was not very serious. It concerned a runaway boy, Stevie, about eight or nine years old. Although in child guidance clinics doctors and social workers usually work separately with the child and the parents, these doctors were experimenting in working with the child and a parent together. When they talked to the father and the child about the little boy's runaway experience, they were struck by the interaction between the two of them. The interaction went something like this: the father said, "Now, Stevie, tell the doctors about the time you ran off on the railroad tracks." Stevie started to say, "Well, I went off from home after my lunch," and the father interrupted, "Yes, and you took your teddy bear." "Oh, yes," said Stevie, "I took my teddy bear. And then I went down the street to the tracks." And the father said, "Remember, the train was coming by, and you decided to follow it along." And so it went on, with the father prompting and encouraging the child in his story, and the child responding to the father's great interest in his travels, until the long story finally ended. Then the father's expression changed, and he said: "You see, doctor, how naughty he is. This is what goes on all the time and there is nothing we can do about it."

What the doctors observed was that the father *was* doing something about it, showing the child clearly how interested he was in the child's misbehavior. They also saw that the father's shift to sternness at the end of the story was a conventional afterthought, which the child really didn't take seriously because he had seen how interested the father was.

The father had been a long-distance truck driver who had taken big semitrailers across the mountains to California. He had loved this work, but, when he got married and started having a family, had regretfully decided that cross-country driving was not a practical occupation for a family man. So he gave up that job and took a nine-to-five job in the city. The idea of traveling around the countryside still fascinated him, and it soon became clear that he was vicariously experiencing through his child the excitement of exploration that he no longer could permit himself, and that the child was responding to his encouragement with more explorations. The father wasn't aware of what he was doing; he had no idea that he had been encouraging his son to run away. He honestly thought that he was trying to keep him from running away by spanking him or by whatever discipline he used.

Although Stevie's escapades were not antisocial, the doctors

soon discovered the same type of sequence in delinquent behavior—stealing and fire-setting and even murder—when it
occurred in families in a conventional middle-class environment. From the case of Stevie, therefore, came what I consider
the most important theory about the cause of the defective
conscience.

It is tempting to use this theory to lay all the responsibility
for a child's misbehavior at the family's door. But the parents
are not consciously trying to corrupt the child; in most cases
their intentions are the best, and they are usually less aware
of their own inner impulses to misbehave than Stevie's father
was of his impulse to travel. Their unsolved problems lead them
to communicate an expectation of misbehavior that weakens
the child's capacity to inhibit the antisocial impulse. Unfortunately, society tends to assume that if you are bad in one way,
you are bad all the way through, and so once one type of misbehavior occurs, society's expectations encourage other kinds
of misbehavior.

According to this way of looking at antisocial misbehavior,
one of Edward's parents, probably his hard-working, conscientious father, has some unsolved problems about antisocial behavior. He condones Edward's behavior; as one of you suggested, he probably says, "I was a rowdy myself at that age,"
implying, "and I wish I still could be, but I can't permit myself
to, so the next best thing is for my son to be rowdy for me."
The father feels so guilty, without knowing why, about his
participation in his son's misbehavior that he has to get him
out of every scrape. He has to relieve him of the consequences
of the misbehavior which he is vicariously enjoying. This
sequence of events occurs in many families, and it is much less
difficult to deal with at seven or eight than it is at twenty.

Most kids steal at some time or another; the crucial deter-
minant of future stealing is the parental response. Let me tell
you about a case which illustrates this point. At the age of ten
or eleven two little boys from well-to-do families were caught

smoking cigarettes they had stolen from the back of a car. The parents of both boys inflicted whatever kind of punishment was in style for that particular age group, and presumably that was the end of it. At least, it was the end of it for one family whose message was: "You've been a bad boy. You should never steal and you're too young to smoke. Don't do it again." With that they assumed that he'd learned his lesson and would not do it again. The family of the other child *said* the same things, but *thought*, "He's a thief, and we'll have to watch him." So from that time on, they watched him: whenever anything was missing, they suspected him; when he went to the store with a dollar to buy something, they always checked carefully to make sure he brought back exactly the right change.

This kind of expectation is easily communicated to a child, and becomes a self-fulfilling prophecy. The child is not fooled; he senses that he is expected to steal, that his parents' picture of him is that of a thief, and this self-concept becomes incorporated into his conscience. This family came to me when the boy was fifteen, and said: "We are in terrible trouble. Our son broke into a neighbor's house and stole a camera." He felt guilty about it, both consciously and unconsciously, so that he "accidentally" left evidence that implicated him. The parents said, "This is the first time we have ever left him alone." I said, "He is fifteen and this is the first time you have ever left him alone? Why?" "We were afraid that something like this would happen," they replied, and they told me about the episode of the cigarettes and their subsequent expectations of their son's future misbehavior.

Why should this family think that their child would turn out to be a thief because he stole a few cigarettes at the age of eleven? They were not stupid; they had the same background as the family whose child did not continue to steal. The other family knew that young children occasionally take things; you discipline them, and they learn from experience. They did not assume that their son would go on stealing, so he incorporated this assumption into his conscience and he didn't steal anymore. The other boy incorporated the parental assumption that he would steal, so he had no protection from the impulse. Consequently, the first time the family left him alone, implying that he had become an adult and was no longer under their direct control, he had no internal controls to protect him, and the first thing he did was to go out and steal something. His inability to control his impulse made him so nervous and so anxious that he immediately was caught—he didn't consciously arrange it, but he made "mistakes" that resulted in his apprehension.

Often these kids behave as if they were looking for the kind of protection against getting into trouble that jail provides. Military service, too, may be sought after for the same kind of protection. Sometimes a rigid pattern of work can provide the protection; the nature of the job seems to set up an external, auxiliary conscience. That is one reason for the careful scrutiny of people's motivation for entering police work, and I imagine the same may apply to some people who want to work in the church. It is difficult for the policeman or the church worker who unconsciously perceives the law or the church as a means of protecting himself from criminal behavior to be objective in the performance of his duties.

CLERGYMAN 1: Often there is only one black sheep in a large family. How does this theory account for that?

DR. ALDRICH: Apparently the parent, again unconsciously, picks one child as a scapegoat, funneling all his own frustrated, delinquent impulses vicariously through one child's behavior. Something, perhaps the child's appearance or his mannerisms, establishes his role as the scapegoat. The mother of an alcoholic youth said to me: "Right from the beginning, when he was a baby, we were worried. He looked so much like Uncle John, and you know what a lush Uncle John is." An adopted child is frequently the scapegoat, partly because of the fantasies adoptive parents have about their child's origins, and partly because it is easy for them to blame misbehavior on heredity and thus exonerate themselves.

Helping the child requires working with the parent as well. The parent needs first to understand and then to change the signals he gives the child. It is not always easy to determine whether mother or father or both are unconsciously contributing to the child's misbehavior. In the case of a sixteen-year-old boy who stole a car, we first assumed that the father was giving the signal. He was a self-righteous pillar of the community and the church, and we had thought he might be covering up some less acceptable impulses; but we couldn't find any evidence that he was encouraging his son's stealing. However, we did find out what was going on between the mother and the boy. The boy was six feet tall—he had grown rapidly and, like most adolescents who grow rapidly, he was hungry 95 percent of the time. His mother was a compulsive person for whom everything had to be just so, including a schedule of three meals a day and no eating between meals. When the boy came home from school feeling half-starved, the mother said: "Don't spoil your dinner. Dinner is at six o'clock." But the boy was hungry right then and thought it was ridiculous to miss a snack when he always ate an enormous dinner anyway, so he began to figure out ways of getting food behind his mother's back. This led to a kind of game in which the mother, instead of saying openly, "Let's talk this over," or "Let's compromise," or "I'll give you an extra sandwich in your lunch," kept trying to keep him from eating. She would hide the cookie jar, and he would find it. She hid the potato chips, and he found them. He did not have too much trouble finding them, because she was a co-conspirator; so was he, or he would have bought a milk shake or something before coming home. She finally put a padlock on the refrigerator, and he picked the lock.

By this time, the game had become deadly serious. To the mother, picking the lock signified stealing, and this stirred up some of her own latent conflicts about stealing; she began to see her son as a potential thief in other areas. Her expectation that he would steal weakened his own confidence in his capacity to resist the temptation to steal, so when somebody left a car with the keys in it, he started off down the road and went into the ditch. He didn't have to drive it in the ditch—he was a good driver—but the feeling of guilt and the need for some kind of outside controls determined his behavior so that he got caught. He acted as if he were saying, "Help me, somebody, to restrict my impulses!"

The defective conscience can originate in community expectations as well as parental expectations. Communities that say, "That boy is going to steal because he is a Negro, or because he is a school dropout, or because he lives in this kind of neighborhood," contribute to the fulfillment of their prophecies.

CLERGYMAN 6: But not all children from slum neighborhoods are delinquent.

DR. ALDRICH: Some parents may counteract the effect of community expectations by their own expectations of conforming behavior. They encourage the development of a conscience that will overcome what the community expects. These parents communicate to their child, "Regardless of what the other kids do, we don't expect you to steal." Their faith may be naïve, but it catches on. And this kind of optimism is essential for anyone who works with delinquent youth. You have to believe that they have the capacity to develop better consciences than they have shown the world.

Returning to Edward's case, the optimism that is needed to work effectively with delinquents doesn't make you a realistic character witness for him; reality and statistics say that since he is at least a two-time loser, he will continue to get in trouble. In fact, it is always difficult to combine the role of character witness with the role of counselor. The same problem makes it difficult for the probation officer to be a counselor and to be responsible for his charge's behavior. It's hard both to trust and to watch someone.

There is another problem in simultaneously counseling and being a character witness for this boy. To counsel him, you have to be completely honest with him and about him, and you have to expect him to be responsible for his actions. He did what he did, and there is no point in pretending otherwise; pretense has already gone too far with his father. Up until now, he has been hitchhiking on his father's responsibility and his father's conscience; in a way he has been doing his father's dirty work, and his father has been paying the bills for it, as though he were making good his son's bad checks. Of course people want to avoid family shame, but as long as father takes the burden on himself of paying for his son's trouble, he encourages the behavior he is trying to overcome.

The role of character witness is too much like the father's attempts to avoid realistic consequences. To counsel Edward, you cannot be associated with anything like that. Only by considering him responsible and by recognizing his responsibility can you begin to help him develop his conscience.

MR. ELLIS: I may still have a choice in this case: I can either be a character witness or I can try to help him by counseling. Are you suggesting that I should choose one or the other, because it is too difficult to do both?

DR. ALDRICH: Yes, I don't think you can straddle this particular fence. It is hard to see what would be gained if you were a character witness for him. As you point out, you haven't known him for long, and you can't say that he didn't do what the court says he did. Even if you decide to be a character witness, and get him off by misrepresenting the real situation, you only purchase relief of the immediate trouble at the expense of later rehabilitation. As you say, the kind of relationship he is looking for is one that will get him out of trouble.

Perhaps you should have a conference with the attorney, in which you make clear to him where you stand and what you think is in the boy's best interests, and warn him that you are not going to compromise yourself. Then it is up to him; if he wants to use you on that basis, he will. You should participate on your conditions, not on theirs. This is hard when you feel so sorry for the family and when you are subjected to so much pressure to fulfill their idea of the pastor's role and to help them avoid family shame. But you have to stand firm on your concept of what is going to be best in the long run, and they have to take it or leave it on that basis.

If Edward asks you to get him out of trouble, it seems to me that you could say: "Look, son, my job is not to get you out of trouble. It is to try to figure out how you got in trouble so you won't get in any more." If he says that it is the fault of "those other guys," you can say to him, "Let's face the fact that you didn't have to be with the other guys." If the court wants to put him on probation to you, I would consider saying: "Look, Judge, I want to help this boy. In order to help him, I have to trust him. If I have to check up on him, it will be hard for me to help him. I might be helpful in a counseling role, but I don't think I can be helpful as a probation officer. I think you should get your own probation officer." You don't have to bail out the judge.

If I decided to try helping Edward through counseling, I would probably begin by asking, "Who first gave you the idea that you couldn't control your temptation to steal?" He may not know right away, but as the two of us explore his early experiences, he will form a reasonably accurate picture of its origin.

Once he identifies the source of his concept of himself as a thief, through father's or mother's expectations, I go on to say, "Are you telling me that, with everybody expecting you to steal, you thought you could not do anything about it?" He probably is quick to agree because he is anxious to assign responsibility to his parents, but I ask, "Why not?" He is surprised, and asks, "What do you mean?" and I say, "Just because other people didn't think you could do anything about it, what made *you* think so?" I suggest to him that he is a sucker to believe father, mother, or whoever intimated to him that he *had* to be a thief. I am saying that *I* don't believe it, and therefore, I am going to hold him responsible for his behavior. I am not going to let him off the hook, although I feel sorry for him because he has been for so long under the misapprehension that he doesn't have a conscience. I let him know that he can have a conscience, and now that he knows he can, I expect him to develop one.

This responsibility will make him nervous, and he may test me. Do I secretly expect him to steal? Do I mean it when I assume that if he says he isn't going to steal, he won't do it? He may even try to trap me into checking up on him. If I discover that he is doing so, I say: "Oh, come on now. We are working together to try to help you figure out what caused this behavior, but you are trying to put me in the same role as your father. I am not going to play that game." I then repeat my expectations that he can and will develop a conscience and does not need checking up on. You can see why I must be genuinely optimistic. I must really trust him, so that if he tells me he has stolen again, I am genuinely surprised and disappointed. I then must go on trusting him, making clear to him my assumption that he can learn from experience and develop an adequate conscience. It is the only way I can be successful with him.

If he is living at home and his family continue to check up on him every time he comes in the house, my trust will be counterbalanced by their distrust. It is discouraging to treat a boy like this while he remains at home, particularly since each problem that arises adds to his family's conviction that his problems will never end. It isn't going to be easy to treat him in jail either, because the whole atmosphere of jail suggests that iron bars are the only way to prevent him from misbehaving. Jail thus encourages misbehavior, and it is not surprising that offenders repeat their offenses. Jail seldom cures delinquency, although it may protect society from the delinquent.

However, you can treat the parents as well as the child. The goal is to enlist the parents to help the child, not to accuse them of causing his misbehavior. In working with Edward's father, you might start by saying, "You have been helping him get out of these scrapes for a long time, haven't you?" "Yes," says the father, "I sure have." "You've gotten discouraged by now, I guess." "I sure am," he says, responding to your understanding attitude. "This goes back a good many years?" "Yes, in sixth grade he first was in trouble." "And each time he has been in trouble, you have helped him avoid the consequences?" "Well, I guess you might say that," says the father, beginning to wonder about it. "I wonder if you have had some question about whether perhaps at some time he might need to suffer the consequences?" He replies, "Well, as a matter of fact, yes." You can then say, "I can see that you kept postponing the evil day." In this way, starting from a question, you have ended in agreement that the father has been protecting the boy more than was good for him. Then he may say, "I suppose I should have let him take the consequences." And, nodding agreement, you say: "Well, it is water over the dam now. The question is, how can we work together to help him build enough of a conscience so that he is protected from more of this?" You have moved from a position as the father's critic to a collaboration with him, and you can work much better with a collaborator than with someone you are criticizing.

You ask him the same question you ask the boy: When did he first find himself expecting his boy to steal? He will probably identify an incident like cigarette stealing in the sixth grade, and you might ask: "You seem particularly sensitive about this incident. I wonder if it had a special significance for you in the light of your own early experience?" If this kind of approach is made in an empathic, uncritical way, the results can be illuminating. In the case of the boy whose mother locked the refrigerator, the mother recalled that as a child she used to steal money; she had tried to stop but couldn't and she still felt guilty about it. When she found her own child stealing, she felt that history would repeat itself and anxiously set about preventing it in the only way she knew; but her efforts only served to perpetuate it.

She was a devoted parent, and when she had discussed her own stealing and her feelings about it, and had found that someone else could accept her even though they knew she had stolen as a child, she began to get her feelings about her son in perspective. With encouragement, she could discuss her concerns more directly with her son, and he could relate his concerns to her. Her expectations of him became more realistic, and he could use help more effectively to plug the hole in his conscience.

Once the conscience hole is plugged, it would be safe to explore the impulse that has been expressed in the misbehavior, but only if it seems necessary to do so. The impulse behind stealing may be simply acquisitiveness, or it may symbolize something else—dammed-up hostility against authority, or a need for a substitute for love, or something like that. Unless the person has built enough of a conscience barrier to prevent their expression, stirring up these impulses by exploring their causes may lead to more behavior problems. Exploring the basis of any symptom usually increases its severity, and the possible consequences of exploration should be carefully considered before it is undertaken.

Now, after all this talk, how do you feel about going back to your parish to work with this family, Mr. Ellis? Have I expected too much of you? I got carried away by the possibilities here and perhaps frightened you off.

MR. ELLIS: At least you have convinced me that I don't want to be a character witness! There might be some things I could do, but I am apprehensive about the tremendous amount of time

I could spend on this problem. Maybe I am getting a little calloused, but there are a lot of other people who need help.

DR. ALDRICH: I'm not sure you would have to spend as much time with Edward as you fear. It's up to you to decide how much time to spend with him. If he shows an interest in counseling, it is worth reaching out to him, at least for an interview or two. This will let him know what you're interested in doing and what you're not interested in doing; then you can leave it up to him.

CLERGYMAN 8: Isn't this case another example of the fine line between minister and psychiatrist? Aren't you encouraging the minister to play the role of the psychiatrist?

DR. ALDRICH: In a way, I guess I am, because I am not sure that Edward will receive any help unless you provide it. Not many psychiatrists are looking for boys like this to treat. Psychiatrists have so many demands on their time that they can pick and choose. They choose to treat the kinds of patients they feel most competent to treat, and few feel as competent to treat behavior problems as they do to treat such conditions as anxiety states and depressions. So I think that you and others who are not psychiatrists will be the ones who will continue to carry out most of the treatment of delinquent youth. As all of us learn more about the problem, the results should be better. In the future I hope that psychiatrists will do more consulting with others who are in direct contact with delinquents.

CHAPLAIN NIGHSWONGER: I have never heard so optimistic an interpretation from a psychiatrist in a case like this. Your description is encouraging in that you don't write these boys off as hopeless cases. But in spite of your reassurance, I felt that if I were the parish pastor, the prospect of treatment would be almost overwhelming. A lot depends on the pastor's skill and insight. Furthermore, a community with a good mental health clinic provides backing and consultation and creates a different situation from one in which the pastor is all alone in his community. All these factors are involved in determining how treatment starts.

CLERGYMAN 1: Recently a man came to see me who had been referred to a psychiatrist by the court. I called the psychiatrist, but he didn't seem too interested, although he said he would call me if there was anything that he thought I should know about. Since I haven't heard from him, I wonder if I should call back and really press it.

The judge had told the patient, "You should go to church every Sunday," which upset me a little. But here he is, he comes to church every Sunday. And I don't know whether the psychiatrist thinks I should leave this man alone outside the usual pastoral relationship or what.

DR. ALDRICH: Perhaps the psychiatrist is on the same kind of spot. I would not be surprised if the judge had said, "Go to church every Sunday and go to the psychiatrist every Tuesday." I am not too happy about this kind of referral either, because although the judge can require a patient to see me, he cannot make him respond or participate in treatment. When a patient says to me: "The judge sent me. What are you going to do about it?" I am as stymied as you are. Perhaps that has something to do with the psychiatrist's lack of interest.

You might call him and say: "Doctor, it looks as if we are both in the same boat. The judge has assigned this man to both of us. I don't know what I am supposed to do and I wonder if you could help me." The psychiatrist might say: "I feel trapped too. I can't treat a patient who is under duress unless he has some feeling that he wants to be here." But between you, you might try to find a way to turn this situation into something helpful.

CLERGYMAN 1: How about talking with the judge, who I think wants to be cooperative?

DR. ALDRICH: Yes, it could be helpful to talk with the judge about the difficulties of acting as an informal parole officer, although it might require a good deal of tact.

CLERGYMAN 7: Where do judges pick up the idea that an involuntary referral to a psychiatrist or to a church can be helpful? Is there something we can do about it?

DR. ALDRICH: I don't know where they picked up the idea about the church, but I am afraid that they picked up the idea about us from us. We've been claiming for a long time that we know how behavior problems and delinquency get started in childhood. Every Sunday there is an article in the paper that tells exactly how delinquency develops and what to do about it, except that the right person is never available. So it's no surprise that some judges say, "O.K., you know so much about them— take them!" I think the psychiatrists have asked for it, but I don't know how you got in the act.

The involuntary character of the judge's referral is only natural, I suppose, because virtually all of his dispositions are made under duress. Perhaps we should be more understanding of the judge's position. He probably does want to be cooperative and to help rehabilitate the prisoner, but he can't create motivation.

Both our professions should be concerned with delinquency, but most of us are handicapped in treatment if the delinquent isn't motivated. Furthermore, not all psychiatrists are comfortable with delinquents or enjoy working with them and they sometimes use the involuntary character of the referral as a rationalization for not making the effort.

CLERGYMAN 1: If I were a psychiatrist, I suppose I could ignore these people. But if a man is a member of my congregation, regardless of how he got there, he is my parishioner, and I cannot slough him off because his motivation isn't just right.

DR. ALDRICH: Yes, you are more involved than the psychiatrist. I can say to the judge, "You can put pressure on the patient if you want, but you cannot tell me what I will do." This approach doesn't make for good feeling between the legal and the psychiatric professions, but I can use it to extricate myself if I choose. But you have a different kind of obligation, because of the ground rules of your profession. I do not believe, however, that your ground rules require you to set up a formal counseling relationship unless you consider that it will be fruitful. I believe that you discharge your obligation by accepting him in your congregation as you accept anyone else, which includes giving him the privilege of seeking counseling from you if he wishes.

Sometimes, however, the apparent impasse can be turned into the beginning of constructive help. When he comes to you saying, "The judge said I had to see you," you might reply, "It sounds to me as if you don't think much of the idea." He can hardly disagree, and you have at least one point in common. Then if you ask, "What do you suppose the judge thought we could accomplish?" he probably won't know, and neither will you, so you have two points in common. As I see it, you try to accumulate enough honest points in common so that he begins to sense some empathy between you. Eventually you may feel that you can risk a statement like this: "Well, it looks as if the judge thinks that together we can learn something about how you got into this mess. You don't think so, and frankly I'm skeptical too, but we seem to be stuck with each other for a while, and since we're stuck, we might as well try to figure out what it's all about." If you are matter of fact and honest, without being critical or condoning, you may have a chance.

If you decide to work with Edward and his father, you may be able to help him plug the hole in his conscience. If you find that his problem is too much for you to handle, you may then have to consider a referral. Some cases like Edward's will require more than you can give them, and I don't think you should feel discouraged if you aren't able to help them all. But Edward has begun to turn to you, and I think you might have a chance of helping him.

Chapter Seven

THE
WITHDRAWN
ADOLESCENT

The case of Frank concerns a father who is threatened by his son's achievements, and the boy's reaction to the situation. The discussion focuses on how Mr. Fox can reach Frank by working with the father, in spite of his dislike for him. The importance of setting limits and of confidentiality in counseling is emphasized. A discussion of the process of referral includes the question of communication between clergymen and psychiatrists.

MR. FOX: Frank is a boy of sixteen who comes from an upper middle-class home. In grammar school he received awards for mathematics and English and he had an excellent scholastic record in high school until last year. A little over a year ago, for the first time in his career, he did not get a prize or even an honorable mention in the city-wide high school photographic competition. At the same time he had difficulties with two or three of his teachers and shortly thereafter he quit school. He retreated from everything, and he has been out of contact with almost everyone since that time.

Frank's father is a boastful person, whose inability to get along with others accounts for the fact that he works for himself rather than for somebody else. He is loaded with ideas but is completely unable to carry them out because he is bragging so much of the time. His boasting is hard on his business, but it is even harder on his social relationships. For instance, he never sees me without bragging about the fact that he doesn't drink, smoke, or swear. He has an excellent mind, and I think that a good deal of Frank's achievement has really been his father's achievement. In his photographic work Frank had complicated equipment that none of the others ever had, and so he could undertake projects that were far beyond the ability of the other youngsters.

Frank's mother doesn't express much affection, at least in my presence, but she doesn't really seem cold. She is somewhat retiring, and I have never heard her say a single word of complaint in any way whatever.

DR. ALDRICH: You sound as if you felt she had plenty to complain about.

MR. FOX: Well, I'm sure she does. She hardly gets a chance to say anything when her husband is around, because as soon as she starts to speak, he immediately takes over the conversation. If you want to talk to her, you have to do it when he isn't around, and that is a little difficult because his business is in the home. Although she does not complain, she always has a wistfulness about her.

Both parents are highly intelligent. Frank's I.Q. is about 130, according to the father, who claims that his own I.Q. is a little higher. The mother went to high school. The father started college but didn't graduate.

Frank is like his father; he is boastful and is unpopular with his peers for the same reasons that his father is unpopular. For the last year, however, he has been withdrawn. He stays at home, reading and developing his films.

I have seen him about fifteen times during the year. At first I couldn't get to see him at all—when I came to the house he went to the bedroom or the basement, and I did not force the matter. In the last four or five months he has at least come out and talked. But the minute I approach the things his parents would like to know, he just stops talking or finds a reason to leave. I don't know how to draw him out or even whether I should try. He probably thinks that I am trying to get information about him for his parents.

DR. ALDRICH: Are you?

MR. Fox: Well, in a way I suppose I am. Not really for them, but Frank undoubtedly recognizes that they have asked me to talk with him and therefore suspects that I will relay to them whatever he tells me.

DR. ALDRICH: What is the parents' attitude toward him? Are they impatient, or cajoling, or lenient, or what?

MR. Fox: Intellectually they acknowledge the doctor's recommendation that they go slow and not push him. On the other hand, it is obvious that they *are* pushing and are impatient with the whole business. I am sure they are conscientiously trying not to, but they just do.

The parents urged him to try to go back to school at the beginning of this semester. He went for a day and a half, and then just came home. He said he "couldn't face them." He didn't say why he couldn't face them or even whom he couldn't face.

His doctor recommended a psychiatrist; Frank went to him once but would not go back. Nobody is helping him right now, and he just sits at home.

DR. ALDRICH: What do you think has happened?

MR. Fox: It seems to me that Frank has always wanted to do something on his own, but he feels that he has never been able to. Everything was his father's doing. When it all began, in the photographic competition, the judges had insisted that the projects should not involve special equipment. Frank had to do it on his own and he was not successful.

CLERGYMAN 1: Does he have any girl friends?

MR. FOX: Goodness, no.

DR. ALDRICH: You say that with feeling.

MR. FOX: He shuns girls altogether. As a matter of fact, he doesn't have many friends of either sex. He has never had even the ordinary friendly relationships that boys and girls have who go back and forth to school together. He has always been picked on by his peers.

DR. ALDRICH: What has the family done about that? Have they projected all the blame onto the other boys, or have they thought that Frank might be partially at fault?

MR. FOX: I suppose they blame the others. The father says, "The other boys are jealous of him," or "He is smarter than they are." Frank has only once been in a fistfight—only once did he really stand up and fight back, and he got a thorough trouncing.

CLERGYMAN 2: Has he had more money than the other kids?

MR. FOX: He has always had money, but he has always seemed a little tight with it.

DR. ALDRICH: With the material we now have, we can hazard a very tentative working formulation of Frank's case. We don't know how much security Frank developed in infancy, but your description of the mother suggests that it was difficult for her to be warm and loving and secure in motherhood. She is subordinated in the home to the aggressive father, whose boasting is probably a way of compensating for feelings of inadequacy. If he really felt adequate, he wouldn't have to advertise it.

Frank is intellectually aggressive or he was until he got taken down a peg. He identifies with his father in his boastfulness.

They both have poor interpersonal relationships, and both are loners to some extent. Father seems to be a pseudoindependent person who can't tolerate working under or being dependent on anybody. The boy identifies not only with the part that father wants him to see but with the whole picture, including his father's inadequacy.

The father probably dominates Frank as well as the mother. If the father can't be subordinate to anyone, he also has to keep the boy from achieving up to his level; he says, "Frank has an I.Q. of 130, but mine is a little bit higher." I suspect that this pattern is true of the entire relationship. Father in effect says, "Do *almost* as well as I do, but see to it that you don't do *as* well." A father who feels inadequate feels threatened by a son who is becoming an adult. A son who is a high achiever is fine as long as he is a little boy, but when he gets close to becoming a man, he becomes too much of a threat. This may be the reason for the son's difficulties in adolescence.

MR. FOX: In the last six months, I have tried to set up two little projects with the boy. In one he developed some pictures for me. While we were working on them, he was just the same as he used to be. But when I took him and his father to a photographic exhibition, the boy never said a word the whole time. At that time I didn't relate it to the fact that his father was there.

DR. ALDRICH: In some way the father may have signaled to the boy that he should not do too well. The father has been supporting him so far, but Frank may now be getting a new message that he should slow down. This double message may be confusing him. He has identified with a father who cannot accept anything but his own superiority, or pseudosuperiority. But the tenuous security that Frank has been trying to build with his father's help may now suddenly be sabotaged by his father. His father no longer gives him the kind of support that will make him the highest achiever but subtly pulls the props from under him.

Frank doesn't have much to do with girls. We don't know that his father is scared of women, but he certainly seems to be. He doesn't let his wife get a word in edgewise and he completely dominates her. A man doesn't have to dominate a woman unless he is afraid that she might dominate him. It is possible that the son is identifying with the father's anxieties about his relationships with women without having the confidence to dominate women himself; this makes him withdraw from the threat of competition and the threat of girls and stay at home. He regresses to the point of giving up being aggressive or self-assertive.

MR. FOX: Why does he isolate himself from everyone? Not only won't he go to school but he won't come to church or to our young people's group. He won't meet the kids on the street. He has one buddy who comes over to his house and they do a few things together, but otherwise he does not have anything to do with anyone outside the family.

DR. ALDRICH: I think he has regressed right past the stage at which friendships and relationships outside the family circle are established. He really didn't do too well in this period; his relationships seem to have been on an intellectual basis, and most of the other kids didn't like him. So he has regressed past the point of emotional investment in the problems of adolescence or in the problems of relationships with friends, and he is back in a narcissistic phase of preoccupation with his own needs.

The fact that he has one buddy, even though he may also be somewhat of an oddball, is a favorable sign.

CLERGYMAN 8: It seems to me that you are reading an awful lot into this case.

DR. ALDRICH: I would certainly be reading too much into it if I viewed what I have said about Frank as anything more than a tentative working hypothesis. The evidence so far is slim, and each part of the hypothesis would need careful testing against historical and current information before I could be at all confident of its accuracy. However, you need a working hypothesis before you start an individualized approach and you cannot wait until you are absolutely certain or you will never start. I am not certain that my formulation is accurate, but I need a starting place to develop my understanding of how Frank's symptoms have come to pass and to develop my strategy of treatment.

CLERGYMAN 2: Do you think he might have to go to a hospital for treatment?

DR. ALDRICH: When I heard the first part of the story, I was afraid that he might be suffering from the beginning of a schizophrenic reaction. Schizophrenia is the most frequent serious illness of young people; it is difficult to treat and usually requires hospitalization. It is characterized by withdrawal and preoccupation with one's self, and it is often seen in late adolescence. The first signs may be a deterioration in school grades: the kid who has been getting B's starts getting C's and D's. Others start with peculiar concerns about health. So far Frank fits the picture. But I don't get the feeling of loss of contact that appears in schizophrenia. He shuts himself off, but you can get through to him.

MR. FOX: Remember that I arranged the situations where we have made contact. He could hardly refuse without being discourteous.

DR. ALDRICH: The severe schizophrenic is trapped by his illness into such profound isolation that courtesy and other social niceties lose their significance for him. The milder schizophrenic may accept the invitation but does not really participate. But there seems to be some involvement in Frank's participation with you. In the photography project he worked naturally with you. The schizophrenic usually can't get involved but sits passive and preoccupied in a situation like that; you can't break through his shell. So my feeling of optimism comes from the fact that after a year of sitting at home, away from people, he is still able to relate to you, and he still has a friend who relates to him. He hasn't withdrawn progressively into his shell to the point where nobody can get to him.

CHAPLAIN NIGHSWONGER: How does this family participate in church life? What religious interests do they have?

MR. FOX: The mother attends church. She belongs to the Women's Auxiliary and comes to most of the usual social affairs. The father comes occasionally and has been rather active in the Sunday school teaching and on the Sunday school committee. Lately, since the boy has dropped out of school, he has not been meeting with the committee because some of them have grown so antagonistic to him that the situation is becoming unpleasant.

DR. ALDRICH: Perhaps he was able to work with other children as long as they were young and as long as his own child was young. But, as his own child becomes adolescent, his control is threatened and he feels more need to show how good he is. When his boasting increases, he antagonizes people more easily, and so it would be consistent with this hypothesis that the father's relationship with children in Sunday school should break down as his son enters adolescence.

MR. FOX: When I first knew Frank, eight years ago, he would leave the room when the father's bragging began to get out of control.

DR. ALDRICH: He was ashamed of his father and yet he identified with him. It is a hostile, angry identification that psychiatrists call "identification with the aggressor." In other words, if
you can't fight 'em, join 'em. His father has always been too
much for Frank, and rather than put up a struggle, Frank
joined him. Frank became the same kind of person, even though
he disliked his father, and so now he dislikes himself. To some
degree, identification with the aggressor is common: someone
may say to you, "I find myself acting like my mother and that
makes me annoyed, because I have always resented this aspect
of her and here I am doing the same kind of thing she does."
The genesis of the identification seems to be back in the three-
to six-year-old period, and it is difficult, though not impossible,
to change later on.

CLERGYMAN 7: What can we do for this boy? He sits at home
and won't go to the psychiatrist, and it is hard to treat somebody you can't talk to. If he sees the psychiatrist and Mr. Fox
as informers for his father, he'd see anyone in authority in the
same light.

CLERGYMAN 3: I wonder how the father felt about the boy going to the psychiatrist. He might have sabotaged the treatment
because he was afraid that the psychiatrist would find out how
Frank's troubles reflected on him.

DR. ALDRICH: You are probably right. The father could be
afraid that he will be exposed. The father may also be afraid
that the boy will improve, although I am sure he is not conscious of that feeling. When an adolescent whose adequacy
threatens his parents begins to get better with counseling or
psychotherapy, the parents become more anxious and may
rationalize taking him out of treatment. Their own neurotic
needs are served by the child's problems, and if the child overcomes his problems, their balance is threatened. For this reason,

and because, as in the case of Edward [Chapter Six] the family can be helpful as well as detrimental to the adolescent's progress, psychiatrists like to have the parents either in a treatment relationship of their own or in family treatment, in which the family is treated as a unit.

Do you know whether the psychiatrist talked to the boy's family?

MR. FOX: He may have talked to the mother because she took Frank to the only interview they had.

DR. ALDRICH: I would guess that the father has found one excuse or another to avoid contact with the psychiatrist.

MR. FOX: He keeps saying he will do anything under the sun to help the boy.

DR. ALDRICH: I would pick him up on that. But I would be careful *not* to imply that he is the cause of it all and must counteract what he has done to his boy. This approach is too threatening, and in spite of all we have said about the father, it is not entirely true. He is a contributor, but not the whole cause and although unconsciously he may sabotage his boy, he is consciously and genuinely concerned about him.

I think I would speak to him in much the same way that I would speak to Edward's father [Chapter Six]. If I were you, I would gradually work up to a statement somewhat like this: "Well, it seems to me that you are the person who can do most to help this boy of yours. I know that you have tried many approaches without success, and I can see that you are about at the end of your rope. Perhaps the first step is for you to get some kind of help for yourself that will make it easier for you to know how to steer Frank to a source of help, since he presumably isn't going to go without assistance from someone." If you can honestly do so, it is always best to respond to the needs of the parishioner as he perceives them than to attempt to superimpose what you perceive as his needs.

I would be in no hurry, however, to get Frank to go to the psychiatrist. I think he might find it too threatening until he sees that his father is involved. Without the father's involvement in treatment, Frank inevitably would perceive the psychiatrist as another dominating parent figure and he is too scared of his father to let anyone else in. Furthermore, if the father were not involved, he couldn't help competing with the psychiatrist. One hour with the psychiatrist versus twenty-three hours with his father is a disadvantage no psychiatrist can overcome in this kind of situation. I think that you will help the boy most by first encouraging his father to get some help with his own feelings. It is therefore no misrepresentation to send him for help so that he can help his boy.

It's possible that Frank's father would be more willing to accept help from you than from me, but in either case the procedure would be about the same. If he did come to see me, I would start by asking him how he accounted for the problem.

MR. FOX: I did, and he blamed it all on the French teacher.

DR. ALDRICH: Teachers are ideal scapegoats for parents to hold responsible for their children's problems. Not that they're never at fault, but teachers don't have the opportunity to cause trouble unless the groundwork has been laid at home. However, I wouldn't argue about it. I would ask him what happened with the French teacher, and I wouldn't be surprised if he projected himself into the teacher's role, and told a story which amounted to saying that the French teacher really can't stand the competition because the boy is so bright.

I wouldn't argue about this explanation, either, but would say after the father had finished: "The problem we have to work on really is not so much the French teacher but the way in which your boy responded to the whole situation. I think we may have to look at more than just what happened at school. He has been out of school for quite a while now." Of course, although I am being somewhat subtle, the father will still get the message that he may be partly at fault and responsible, particularly if he feels guilty about his role. I would try to help him focus more on his worries than on his guilt about the boy, so that he could work toward developing more understanding of their relationship and of how it might be used to better advantage in helping Frank. To be successful, I would have to be honestly interested in the father; I would have to overcome my dislike for this irritating character who is always bragging about how good he is.

MR. FOX: I confess that, for me, working with the father takes an exceedingly conscientious effort. I haven't avoided it, but it is something I wish I could avoid.

DR. ALDRICH: It is important to recognize that you don't like him. If you feel so guilty about not liking someone that you have to pretend to yourself that you do like him, you avoid facing your feelings about him, and you become much less helpful to him. Unfortunately, the people who need the most help are often people who are unpleasant to spend time with. That is one reason why it is essential to set limits to the time you spend with this man.

Setting limits to your interview is an important consideration in any case, for several reasons. In this case, keeping yourself from getting fed up is a significant and legitimate reason. If you know that in ten minutes or twenty minutes he will leave, he is much easier to put up with than if you think, "Gosh, I don't know how I'll ever get rid of him," as you go on and on and on. Even though you don't operate on a schedule, I think with someone like this you should ask him to come in and talk with you for a specific period of time, say forty-five minutes. When he comes in at ten thirty you can say, "O.K., we've got until a quarter after eleven." At a quarter after eleven, you don't have to say, "I've got other things to do," but you can say: "Well, I think we are beginning to get some understanding of this. Why don't you come in next week?" If he says, "Yes, but I haven't finished; I have more to tell you," you can say, "Fine, we can talk some more about it next week." If he still insists on talking, you pleasantly but firmly get out of your chair, go to the door and open it, and walk out with him, if necessary, in order to make sure that he knows that it is the end of the session.

In order to set limits this way, both of you must know that there will be another session later on. If you can limit each session, you are less inclined to find an excuse not to see him next week.

CLERGYMAN 6: Do you always try to be interested in the people you see, or are there times when you are coldly professional in your relationship? Are there certain types of emotional problems where you need not demonstrate warmth?

DR. ALDRICH: Psychoanalysis or intensive psychotherapy can be complicated by too much warmth on the part of the psychiatrist, although I think that coldness is also a handicap. The psychoanalyst tries to be neutral rather than cold, although sometimes neutrality may appear cold. In the kind of treatment or counseling that I have been discussing with you, you do not have to be so concerned about neutrality, although too much warmth may imply a willingness to take over someone's problems. Any counselor is interested, and should appear to be interested, but you should not appear to be the all-protective father who will take over their responsibilities.

There have been people I have disliked too much to help, but there are not too many of them. If my first thought is, "Oh, Lord! Must I put up with Mr. Jones today?" I say to myself: "What is it that is specifically troubling me about Mr. Jones today? Is it my inability to help him as much as I'd like to? Or is it something else?" This bit of introspection is usually enough to rekindle my interest in Jones and his problem. If it isn't, I wonder whether I am doing him any good. I need a goal in helping him solve his problem, and my interest in reaching this goal makes up for the personal annoyance I may feel. I think that if you set yourself a goal in this case, you will feel that you are accomplishing more than *just* listening to Frank's father's boasting. You may have to listen to a certain amount of boasting, and it may be essential for you to do so to let him protect himself from the blow to his self-esteem that his need for outside assistance constitutes. If you are interested in his problem, you don't have to be very fond of him as a person.

In Frank's case I am assuming that I am interested in the father, although I don't like him very much, and that I can limit the amount of my time he takes. Let's also assume that I have been successful in helping him overcome his tendency to project all the responsibility for Frank's troubles onto the French teacher. As he discusses other aspects of his son's life, I will gently encourage him to look at some of the similarities between his son and himself. After he reinforces that idea, I'll suggest that understanding himself may help him understand his son. We then will explore some of his background to learn how he became the person he is. In the course of that exploration, if I am not too critical, he will probably tell me some of his concerns about his interpersonal relationships. When he tells me that other people are jealous or envious of him, I will not respond, because I do not want to reinforce his projection of these feelings by emphasizing it. Instead I will respond to anything he says that indicates loneliness or tension, so that he will be encouraged to focus the conversation on himself. I will try to respond either to the part of him that is suffering or to the part of him that is like the boy, doing so at first with comments that reflect his feeling, such as "This still makes you feel lonely."

Later I will relate his feelings to his son's with a comment like, "It must really touch home then, when you see how lonely your son is." In this way I show him that I am trying to understand both of them. I can approach this in more than one way; for example, in connection with the pressure the father exerts to push the child into social contacts, I may say, "I wonder if the pressure you feel about Frank's social life has something to do with your feelings about your own social relationships." If I have timed this comment appropriately, so that he does not have to deny his problem in this area, he will agree. I can then convey to him my recognition that it is hard not to put pressure on a boy when you have so much internal pressure yourself.

In this way I try to help the father understand his response to anxiety about his own inadequacy and how his response intensifies the boy's problem. I also help him understand how his inability to form good relationships is communicated to his son, and how that communication can scare the boy about his own relationships. Thus he and I can arrive at a mutual understanding that our main concern is to reduce the pressure on the boy, and that this concern involves the father's problems.

I have condensed the process—it may take several interviews to get this far—and I have assumed that it progresses relatively smoothly along the lines I have predicted. We may get sidetracked along the way, but if we don't, we are now ready to start talking about his feelings. I expect that he has reacted to this phase of our talks with anxiety and some depression as his defenses against his basic inadequacy are shaken up. As we discover how depressed and anxious and inadequate he feels, he may complain that there is nobody at home he can tell his troubles to. If he does not bring it up spontaneously, I will ask him whether he shares his problems with anyone besides me, and expect that he will say that he cannot.

In either case I will _gently_ suggest that one of the reasons that he has nobody to talk to is that he has built up a wall against letting anybody communicate with him. I am the first person to whom he has let himself communicate his problems. What about his wife? What stands in the way of his sharing problems with her? I have suggested to you that unconsciously he perceives her as a threat, just as everybody seems to be a threat to him; but, although I may make this assumption, he does not see it that way. He may complain that he has always wanted to communicate with his wife, but that she isn't able to. "How does she feel about it?" I ask. He speculates somewhat inconclusively about how she feels, and may then realize that he has contributed to building the wall between them. I then gently suggest that he originally considered me a threat to him, but here I am, a person in authority, working with him and I am *not* threatening him.

Through the encapsulated experience of treatment, I show him that he can communicate with someone if he wants to without having to protect himself by boasting or bluster. I have tried to cope with his bluster, not by countering it with more bluster, but by being interested in the person rather than the protection. It is the same way with the patient who protects himself, unconsciously, by physical complaints. If I am too interested in the physical complaint, responding to it with further questions and more tests, the patient continues to focus on his body. If I show him that I am primarily interested in his life situation, he tells me more about that.

Another approach to the communication problem is counseling the father and mother together. To set this up, I would respond to his speculations about his wife's reaction to their lack of communication by saying, "Perhaps one of the real problems is that just you and I are talking about it; maybe all three of us ought to discuss it." I haven't forgotten the boy, but I think he would indirectly benefit from improved communication between the parents. If they wonder why they're on the spot, and not the boy, I tell them. I might say: "You know, one thing that seems to stand in the way of Frank's progress is his concept of what it means to be an adult. And part of that problem reflects his view of the relationship between you two, so let's talk about it." I try to help the parents to communicate better by making observations as they talk together in my office.

For example, I may suggest to him, "It looks as though your tendency to douse any idea that isn't yours is keeping you from really communicating"; or, to her, "Your ideas come out so apologetically that they invite depreciation, and that seems to be keeping this conversation from making progress."

Eventually, as the two of them work together to iron out their communication problems, the boy may begin to feel less threatened at home. I think he can begin to move outside the family, to take the next step up.

MR. FOX: This is helpful. I get an inkling of how you would help the boy through the parents. If he finds a new relationship with his father and mother, he can relate better to others, and perhaps can make the decision to go back to school.

DR. ALDRICH: I'm not sure I would put it in such concrete terms. By setting up his going back to school as the primary goal, you may inadvertently be putting too much pressure on Frank to move in the directions that you think are good for him. He is going to have to make his own choice concerning the ways in which he begins to branch out.

CHAPLAIN NIGHSWONGER: Meanwhile, can this boy be helped to move back up the ladder through groups in which his father isn't participating? Sunday school might have been helpful, had Dad not been involved.

DR. ALDRICH: Perhaps. I think I would make groups available, but I don't think I would try to push him into them. I would prefer to see him go at his own pace, starting with a group of two: you and the boy or the boy and his friend. I would not expect a return to school before next year.

CLERGYMAN 4: Is there likely to be trouble later on? After you have worked things out with the parents and have everything set up for the boy to be helped by them, and your therapy ends, and your involvement is over, will the father relapse and produce a hostile environment for the boy again so that the whole problem recurs?

DR. ALDRICH: I am afraid that the relapse rate is distressingly high in any psychotherapy. Anyone who gives up smoking knows how easy it is to relapse. It is worth the effort, however, because even a short period of successful adjustment encourages the patient or client to believe that he can make it again.

I would continue with this family until Frank is well established back at school. Before he returns, I would like to talk with him, in this case preferably alone. I think he would accept the idea since his parents have participated. I would be careful not to be too probing about the past, or too critical of his parents, focusing instead on his apprehensions and expectations about returning to school. I would recognize his embarrassment at having been gone so long and indicate my understanding that, as in his previous return, he would find himself out of it for a while.

CLERGYMAN 1: Would it be helpful to form a group for the father and mother with other parents with similar problems? The church seems a natural place for groups to work together; by sharing their feelings of inadequacy, they might help each other.

DR. ALDRICH: Group therapy can be helpful in many situations, but I think it may not be the best approach to this family. This father could easily break up any group by trying to dominate it, just as he did with the Sunday school committee. Although theoretically he would be helped by a group of people with the same troubles, I am afraid that he would protect himself with his usual bluster to such an extent that the group would extrude him or break up before he had a chance to find out that they could help him. Keep in mind that although you may be able to help him with his communication problems within his own family, you are not going to effect a complete personality change in him; he will still probably behave the same way in social situations. The professional person can cope with his own response to this kind of behavior because he is prepared for it, but another person with the same family problems isn't prepared to put up with it.

Another difficulty is that church groups are hard to start for people who are ashamed of their problems. Since the members have contact outside the group, confidentiality is hard to guarantee.

CLERGYMAN 6: Would you recommend that Frank live away from home?

DR. ALDRICH: That's an alternative that should be seriously considered if the father can't be reached. It would be tough on the boy, because he probably hasn't any other source of security. Generally I think it is best to work out a problem like this one with the boy living with his parents, if it is at all possible.

CHAPLAIN NIGHSWONGER: What about a private school, where the boy would be away from people he knew and would be protected from embarrassment?

DR. ALDRICH: That's a possibility, as he begins to think about a return to school. It would depend on the specific circumstances and on how the family felt. I wouldn't want to commit myself before I saw how things were going with his father and mother. I doubt that Frank could make it at this point in a boarding school or any other kind of school. Later the family can decide, with the assistance of the psychiatrist or the pastor or whoever is helping them.

CHAPLAIN NIGHSWONGER: If the decision is to refer the father to a psychiatrist, what are the chances of his getting into treatment and staying with it if he gets there?

DR. ALDRICH: I am tempted to hedge on this one and say that the chances of his getting to a psychiatrist depend on the skill of the person who refers him, and the chances of his staying with it depend on the skill of the psychiatrist who treats him. I can't give you any other honest answer. The referral is a crucial process. The referring person must work with the father to nurture his motivation and overcome his resistance. You must control the temptation to try to force him, because pressure, especially when it implies that the problem is his fault, builds up more resistance against the referral. The strategy of referral requires you to see him and respond to him as a person who potentially can help Frank solve his problems through professional guidance. If a father like this were referred to me, I would want to communicate with the referring person.

MR. FOX: You *would?*

DR. ALDRICH: Yes. Are you surprised?

MR. FOX: That's the first time in my experience with psychiatrists that I've heard such a statement. They don't want to know anything! They will handle it all themselves!

CLERGYMAN 8: I find that most referral agencies are that way. Once they have made the contact, they cut you off.

DR. ALDRICH: I would want to know what you know about this father *before* I see him. However, once I have seen him, I may not want to communicate with you. This is always a problem with referrals. You knock yourself out to get this man to go to the psychiatrist, and now that he has finally gotten there, you don't get any feedback. It is frustrating for you; but remember, this man has made a lifework out of covering up his own feelings of inadequacy because he feels so ashamed of them. As a psychiatrist, I ask him to reveal his inadequacy, very slowly, within a professional relationship. It is enough for him to share his feelings of inadequacy with me, and perhaps with his wife, without asking him to share them with outsiders. He might be scared off if he thought that I would share what I have found out with someone whom he, or his wife, sees every Sunday. How can he return to the Sunday school committee if he thinks that you know all about him? Even if I assure him that I will tell you just enough to let you know how he is doing, he will be upset. He will project his own feelings about himself onto you and assume that you are equally critical of him. So you see, I've got problems enough because he is so ashamed to come to me, and to make it work, I almost have to sign a pledge not to communicate with you at all. When he has overcome some of his apprehension, *he* may be able to tell you about it, but I can't risk telling you.

Sometimes psychiatrists rely too much on this rationale and use it as an excuse for avoiding legitimate communication, but in this case I believe it is justified. If I were seeing him, I would try to make my position clear to you when you make the initial communication by saying, "You know, once I start seeing him, you won't hear much from me about him, because I think it would be too much of a threat to him." Even though indirectly you know what it is all about, he needs to be sure that he hasn't exposed his weaknesses to you. If he were working with you instead of me, he would expose his weaknesses at his own pace as he gauged your response. Since he is telling them to me, he can't judge your response, and therefore cannot correct his fear that you will be critical or rejecting, or both. If I were seeing Frank, I would have to be equally careful about talking with his family. Sometimes it is difficult for the adolescent's family to understand the importance of so strict an adherence to confidentiality. But you can understand that, if an adolescent is to trust me enough to establish communication, he needs to be sure that I am not in league with his parents or other adults, and that I will respect the confidentiality of what he says to me.

When I talk with you before I see the father, I particularly want to know how you have structured the referral. I am less concerned with the details of the family history, since I will get that data anyway. I am also less concerned with your theory about what is going on, because I will have to build my own theory. In fairness to my patient, I should not come into our relationship with too many preconceptions about his troubles. The same applies to patients who are referred to me by other psychiatrists; I must work primarily within my own frame of reference. So your theory about him is of interest but not crucial. What is crucial is how he moved from approaching you to coming to me.

To send him to a psychiatrist who is a member of the church may handicap you. Some people say they want a psychiatrist of the same religion, but it often works out better if the psychiatrist belongs to a different church. The patient may need to feel that there is a social barrier between him and the psychiatrist before he can expose his weaknesses. He would be embarrassed to see the psychiatrist outside the professional situation and he may use this embarrassment as a way to protect himself from the shame of exposing his feelings. It may be easier for him to accept his pastor as a counselor than a psychiatrist who is a member of the congregation and so, in that context, on the same level. On the other hand, parishioners are not always comfortable in a counseling relationship with their pastors. For example, this consideration may have contributed to Chris's tendency not to attend Mr. Cook's church services [Chapter Four].

But Mr. Fox sounded as if he had had a very unsatisfactory experience with a psychiatric referral.

MR. FOX: I was thinking of one case in particular. It took me about six months to get this person to the point of accepting help that was, I know, beyond my ability. When he finally accepted help, I felt a sense of accomplishment. In this instance, I had to make the appointment with the psychiatrist, and asked him whether I could be of help with background information. "No, thanks," he said, and that was it. All the work I had done had gone out of the window as far as the psychiatrist was concerned. Fortunately, this kind of experience hasn't happened often.

DR. ALDRICH: Even once is too much. You felt deflated and angry, and properly so. I think you deserved at least an explanation for his lack of interest in your information. Perhaps he was troubled because you had to make the appointment. Psychiatrists usually hesitate to take on patients for psychotherapy who need to have someone else make the first appointment. It suggests that the incentive may not have come from the patient; if he does come in, he may resent any evidence that you have given information about him. He wants to present his problem to me at his own pace, as he perceives my response. Even if he comes on his own, he may feel that prior information may prejudice me in some way, and so some psychiatrists prefer not to have the kind of information you would like to provide. In any case, however, you are entitled to an explanation.

CHAPLAIN NIGHSWONGER: There's a difference between psychiatrists and the clergy in the goals and in the kinds of rewards of this kind of work. We work in terms of continuing relationships and ongoing programs, rather than relationships terminated when a specific goal has been achieved. I'm not sure that psychiatrists understand some of our anxiety over this problem. And we don't understand the psychiatrist's detached attitude toward what happens as long as he functions appropriately within the limits of his professional role.

DR. ALDRICH: Yes, there is a big difference. This man is part of your congregation—your family, as it were—before, during, and after his treatment; his contact with me starts completely fresh, and I don't expect to see him again after his treatment has ended. I also don't expect much in the way of personal gratification through his gratitude. If a patient says to me: "Oh, Dr. Aldrich! You have done so much for me! I appreciate it so much!" I wonder if the job really has been done; I am afraid that he sees me rather than himself as the person who has achieved our goal. On the other hand, when a patient who is leaving wonders if he could not have dealt with his problems by himself, I have to stifle the urge to say, "Oh, no, you couldn't; you needed good old Dr. Aldrich," because that would tear down his confidence in himself.

CLERGYMAN 1: This is easier when he pays your bill.

DR. ALDRICH: That's so right. The money makes it easier to give up the gratification that comes from the feedback. So my relationship with him is almost a business relationship, whereas he is part of your family. You've got more of a personal investment in him than I have, and I may seem to be rather detached.

CLERGYMAN 2: He is also Exhibit A before our entire constituency; our results with him are exposed to view. So I think that we have some anxieties that you don't face.

DR. ALDRICH: That's right, you are out in front of everybody, and I am not. I imagine that it is much more difficult for you to maintain strict confidentiality than it is for me. My next patient not only doesn't know the last one, but doesn't want to know him.

CLERGYMAN 8: Doesn't the personal involvement that we have in people limit the amount of help that we can give them?

CLERGYMAN 5: Either we limit our help or we risk losing them. I think that if Mr. Fox worked with Frank's father and was successful, he might leave the church. Mr. Fox would know too much about him, and he would be too ashamed of himself. Some of the people I thought I had helped left the church because I became a threat to them. This puts me in a vulnerable position, because people within the congregation say, "You should have been out making calls instead of spending your time with this family, and it didn't do any good at all." I am not sure it didn't do any good just because they have left the church, but this is the evaluation that the parish puts on it.

DR. ALDRICH: I am not sure that I have a good answer for that one, because I'm not in your shoes. There may be an analogy, however, with your efforts to overcome a person's shame at having to seek psychiatric help. If you encourage him to discuss his feelings about a return to the conventional parishioner relationship, and if your response is sufficiently empathic, he may be less ashamed and less likely to leave.

CLERGYMAN 4: I'm not so sure that everyone in the congregation knows what's going on in the counseling ministry. You don't get referrals from within the church. In other words, few people say to their friends, "Take your problems to the minister because he did me a lot of good."

DR. ALDRICH: Even when someone does tell everybody about his treatment, it may backfire, because he does it in such a way that people become uncomfortable and don't want to appear to resemble him. Counseling must be a very private function of the ministry—the parishioner doesn't talk about it, and you can't talk about it. Ideally, even your wife and secretary shouldn't know whom you counsel, and certainly nothing at all about the subject matter. A well-meaning and apparently innocuous remark, such as "I'm glad you're doing so well," from your wife or secretary is enough to start your parishioner on the road to another church.

Another risk is the sermon. Of course, to use a parishioner's problems in a sermon in such a way that the source can be identified is inexcusable, but even if thoroughly disguised, or even if you make up examples, your counselee may wonder when his turn is coming. Even if you make it clear to him that you never use actual examples in your sermons, he may read his own problems into what you say. The same applies to using the example of one case to make a point with another. Doctors can get away with it (though they probably shouldn't) because their patients don't all belong to the same congregation. It's an occupational hazard for you that we don't have.

I think that in the case of Frank and his father you should try to talk with each of them separately, making sure that you maintain confidentiality with each. Although I have suggested that the best way to help Frank is through helping his father, Frank may be more willing to relate to you than I have assumed. On the other hand, if you do work with the father, you may find that Frank will respond without any treatment for himself. You cannot even be sure that the mother is not a significant factor in this case. In any counseling situation you should be flexible enough to adapt to any new elements that may appear.

Chapter Eight

ALCOHOLISM

Some aspects of alcoholism and its relationship to dependency are explored in this chapter. Gail, an alcoholic, and Helen, the wife of an alcoholic, illustrate two common manifestations of the hostile dependent ties associated with alcoholism. The discussion centers on how the pastor can help his overly dependent parishioners without becoming trapped by their excessive demands.

MR. GRAY: Gail is a white woman who is now twenty-seven years old. She married at nineteen and lived with her husband for about three years. He then left her because she had a child by a Negro man. Her family completely disowned her and the child as well. Presumably because she had no other way to care for the child, she has been living in a common-law marriage with another Negro man for the last four years.

He is an alcoholic who abuses her and beats her up, but she works every day to help support him. She says she is fed up with him, yet she is so afraid of him that she does not dare leave and in moments of depression she resorts to drink. When she has had a few drinks, no matter what hour of the day or night, she picks up the telephone and talks to anyone who is willing to listen. Since I am not one who is willing to listen late at night or in the small hours of the morning, I usually terminate the talk rather abruptly.

Gail says she would like to start over again and all that, but, as I mentioned before, she fears that this man will take it out on her if she leaves him. On the other hand, she is a very dependent individual who needs other people on whom she can lean. So she finds herself alone in a world that doesn't really care and she tries to drown her problems in drink.

Sometimes she comes to my office and goes through the same story. I try to convince her that I will stand by her, but that I can't separate her from the man she is living with. She keeps saying she's afraid to leave him; but if she ever did leave him, I would be willing to bet that within another couple of months, she would be living with someone else. She is the kind of person who is always finding ways to punish herself.

DR. ALDRICH: There are many people with that character trait. The tendency to seek punishment is ordinarily called *masochism;* it is the opposite of *sadism,* which is the term for a tendency to punish others. These words came from the names of the Marquis de Sade, who obtained sexual gratification out of giving punishment, and the Baron Masoch, who enjoyed receiving it. Originally these terms referred only to sexual disturbances associated with punishment, but they have since been applied to more general patterns of behavior. The masochistic person continually gets himself into situations in which hostility is directed at him, often by a sadistic person. The two are tied together by the complementarity of their personalities; sometimes their roles are reversed so that the masochistic person becomes temporarily sadistic, and vice versa. The masochistic person acts as though he feels guilty about his own tendencies to be sadistic and so feels that he deserves punishment. Then, making a virtue of necessity, he begins to enjoy the punishment. In addition to being dependent, therefore, Gail seems to be masochistic.

The source of her masochism is necessarily obscure without a history of her early life. One facet of her adult adaptation, however, makes me suspect that she may still be emotionally overinvolved with her father. Currently she is living with one Negro, and she had an affair with another while she was mar-

ried. The average white American family, of which Gail's
family seems to have been representative, considers the Negro
culturally inferior but sexually superior, or at least more potent
and aggressive than the white. If Gail carried an unresolved
attachment to her father into adolescence, when affectionate
ties acquire an adult sexual component, she would have felt
guilty about the sexual aspect of this attachment. Her guilt
could have led her to feel that she deserved punishment and
might also have made her try to separate her sexuality from
her affection, so that she would feel less guilty about her continuing tie to her father.

Gail would not be aware or conscious of the specific nature
of these feelings, but they could influence her behavior. If this
hypothesis were confirmed, her behavior would become easier
to understand. Establishing a relationship with a partner who
is perceived as brutal, potent, and culturally depreciated would
both satisfy her masochistic need for punishment and reinforce
her need to keep sexuality and affection separate.

This theoretical formulation depends on the assumption that
Gail cannot fuse her affectionate feelings and her sexual feelings and thus cannot enjoy sexual relations with someone she
loves. We don't know much about her marriage, except that
it didn't work out. Her sexual adjustment with her husband
may well have been poor, unless he too was a depreciated
person. She ran off to have a sexual life with a depreciated man,
and in doing so cut her ties to her family as well as her ties to
her husband.

Gail's hypothetical persistent tie to her father may in part
explain why she looks for help to a clergyman, who would be a
father substitute for her and who makes it easier for her to
maintain her dissociation of love and sex. You are the good
father-person, firmly set on a pedestal, to whom the good and
pure part of her can relate; the bad, sexual, punishment-need-
ing part of her stays tied to the man she fears. The inconvenient
timing of her calls for help may in part reflect hidden anger at

you—at the substitute for the father whom she loves but who angers her because he has never responded with the complete devotion that she wanted from him.

MR. GRAY: Gail says that the child loves her very much, and even likes her boyfriend, in spite of the friction in the "family." And, come to think of it, there's a note of competition between Gail and the child over the boyfriend.

DR. ALDRICH: I wonder whether she might be afraid that her daughter will do what she wanted to do; if she wanted to take father away from mother, she would now fear that her child would take her boyfriend away from her.

It might at first seem strange that Gail anchored herself to the situation by keeping her child, instead of giving it up for adoption. One reason may be that part-Negro children are not easy to place in adoption. She probably also feels so guilty that she must tolerate the shame of caring for the illegitimate child. Another reason may be related to her dependency and her difficulties in finding someone to depend on. Her family has disowned her; her husband threw her out; the father of her child disappeared. She may have concluded that the only human being she can count on not to desert her is one she can control, and whom can she control better than a baby? As long as the daughter is helpless, she cannot desert Gail. For this reason a dependent woman may insist on keeping an illegitimate child. Unfortunately, she may try to keep the child indefinitely under her control. The child looks to the mother to fulfill her dependent needs, and the mother looks to the child for the same; each wants to receive and neither can give. As a result, the mother becomes the child's rival rather than someone the child can depend on. This rivalry could be contributing to the competitiveness you noted in the relationship of Gail and her child to the boyfriend.

Freud called dependency needs "oral" needs, because, in the

child's earliest period of life, his contact with those on whom he is dependent is primarily with his mouth, through the nursing process. His earliest social relationships, therefore, are structured around oral contact with the mother or whoever represents her. Some later social behavior seems to be derived from this early oral relationship. Taken out of the usual romantic context, a kiss is an oral contact whose similarity to the infant's approach to the breast or bottle is not difficult to perceive.

If satisfaction of oral or dependent needs is not consistently available from human sources, the individual may fall back on a substitute that is symbolically related to the early source of affection. Food—a substance that is orally ingested—may become the symbolic substitute for the provider of food. Food is most important as a solace for dependent people when their needs for love are greatest, as when they become depressed. This pattern is often seen in people who are overweight. They seem to fall back on the substitute instead of the source of real affection because they are basically afraid that other people will reject them if they let themselves be as dependent as they wish to be.

Alcohol is a special kind of food. It performs two functions at once, providing an "oral" but impersonal substitute for affection and, at the same time, numbing the needs for affection through a chemical effect that reduces anxiety. It is not surprising that it is an attractive substitute. Gail probably finds it hard to make contact even with people who might help her unless she has used alcohol to reduce her anxiety about relationships. Only under these circumstances can she ask for or, more likely, demand help. At those times, she is difficult to deal with; on the other hand, if you wait until she is sober, she is unable to come to you for help. So she oscillates between two equally unsatisfactory solutions.

Alcoholism generally occurs in people who are overly dependent, but who find it hard to trust other people enough to let them try to help. They are not easy to help, and usually put the clergyman or physician through a testing period before letting him try. Often it is the alcoholic's wife or husband who comes for help, and this person usually has emotional problems of his own. Mr. Howe's case is an example of such a situation.

MR. HOWE: Helen is a middle-aged woman. Her second marriage was to an alcoholic husband. They have been married about fifteen years during which she has continually nagged him about his drunkenness and continually checked up on him, both on the job and at the tavern. She says: "I *have* to check up on him, otherwise he will spend all his money. He won't come home with a penny."

Helen tells me that he deceived her into marrying him. She says she thought he was sober and didn't drink, but on the day of the marriage he was dead drunk. She says, "All of a sudden I found out what everybody else seemed to have known all along." However, before they were married they did a good deal of drinking together, so she must have known about his habits. She used to drink quite a bit herself, although she quit some time ago.

She was married previously, with children who are now grown up. He also was married before; Helen says that he abused his first wife with no care or concern for her health.

Helen is always ill and always claims that she is on the verge of dying. I think she uses her illnesses to justify staying with her husband. Two or three times a year she leaves him to get a job; she works about a week, but then she develops an illness and has to quit. She says she would leave him, but she can't hold a job, and has to stay with him because she is too sick to work. She is fearful that he might sell the trailer in which they live and leave her flat. Her constant refrain is, "I wish the Lord would hurry up and take me and get me out of all this mess."

Helen seems to be a religious person, with a very sensitive conscience. Any indication that she might be doing wrong upsets her, and she never seems to forgive herself. However, she is not able really to accept what the church can do for her, or what peace can come to her through prayer.

She never speaks of her husband with any affection. She demands that he take her to church; if he is able to drive the car at all, she gets him up, and he brings her to church. Either she can't drive or she won't. She keeps complaining: "He's so drunk he can't help himself. Why does he do this to me?"

If I had to live with her, I'd probably drink too. But she also seems extremely protective of him. When he is stopped for staggering or for driving all over the road, she begs the police to let him go, promising to get him home and take care of him.

Helen was going to send her husband to a hospital but changed her mind. "I just couldn't let him be in there. He would lose his job," she said; but she also says he can't keep a job, although he works regularly, and at the same time claims that she stays with him only for the support.

Helen says she does not need help; however, she wants me to work on him all I can. She has not been too demanding of me, but she does call people in the congregation, and talks with them for hours on the phone. I am glad she doesn't call me.

Her husband has never admitted any problems to me. Neither of them takes responsibility for anything that's wrong, but always blames the other. They are just like three or four other couples I have in my congregation.

DR. ALDRICH: Each blames the other, and each tries to get you to play the role of referee. She says it is his fault, he says it is her fault; each projects the responsibility on to the other. She sees herself as taking a terrible beating, but beneath her masochism is hostility. She feels guilty, and so feels that she deserves punishment, but she is hostile nevertheless.

Yet she is dependent on him as well. In her relationship to her husband, Helen recapitulates an earlier period of life in which relationships are structured in terms of anger and helplessness. I think that his relationships are structured in the same terms, because he does the same kind of thing. For example, on Sunday morning he gets up to drive her to church! She says, "All I need from you is a meal ticket, but get up and drive me to church." He doesn't say, "If you want to go to church, go yourself." Although he probably feels angry, he does what she wants because he needs her too.

Of course, she has some leverage because she can't drive the car. People who don't learn to drive have to be dependent on others to drive them, and this circumstance can become a lever to force others to take care of them.

Thus, each is dependent on the other. In a way Helen resembles Gail, who seemed to be dependent on her helpless infant because only an infant needs her so much that he cannot get away; Helen can only let herself be dependent on a drunk and reasonably helpless husband who cannot get along by himself. If he tries to go on the wagon, to become better able to care for himself and so potentially more independent, she may fear that she will lose her hold on him. She may then begin to push him off the wagon. Often without realizing what she is doing, the wife of an alcoholic may encourage him to drink, sometimes even by taunting him with his inability to drink. In various ways Helen may try to push him back into a position of helplessness, so that she can again have someone more helpless than herself on whom to depend. If he held out and did not resume drinking, she could become terribly anxious and apprehensive. The marriage might break up, or she might go back to drinking.

MR. HOWE: Once when she told me she was going to leave him and go out and get a job, I tried to encourage her; but she retreated almost immediately.

DR. ALDRICH: You see how strong are the ties between two such angry, dependent people, each trying to maneuver the other into a more helpless position. When she checks up on him, it is not with a conscious effort to keep him drinking, but the result is so obvious that you suspect her motives. On Sunday morning when he is sober, his aggression is inhibited and his need to conciliate her is considerable—otherwise he would tell her, "Take the bus or walk to church!"

Their mutual dependency may explain why he stays with her and why she stays with him—why he married her and why she married him. She may have married him in part because her children were beginning to move away and she had nobody to be dependent upon. We don't know the details, but it is possible that her clinging so antagonized them that they cut the ties completely.

MR. HOWE: Her children have very little to do with her.

DR. ALDRICH: So she has to find another child, as it were, or another person she can control, and the best way to control him is to keep him helpless and sodden with drink.

On the other hand, they may have a better potential for improvement than it appears. Looking at the positive side, you might be able to help them if you weren't too ambitious. You wouldn't have a chance if you tried to change their personalities radically, but you might help them to meet each other's needs without being so destructive of each other. That alone would be difficult, but it might be worth a try.

MR. HOWE: Should I see husband and wife together?

DR. ALDRICH: That's one way of approaching the problem, perhaps the best alternative in this case. If you do, you will have to be careful not to take sides; each will want you to join him against the other. You need to interpret their efforts to recruit you rather firmly, to help them focus on the interaction between them.

In working with a couple in conflict, I first try to define their mutual goals—not that he should quit drinking and she should quit nagging, but their earlier goals of a harmonious marriage, mutual affection and support. I try to engage them in a collaborative exploration of their attempts to reach these goals. This exploration helps bring out the positives—their attraction for each other, the basis for their marriage. I would try to help each one tell the other what he liked about him.

I think that this technique is the best way to break down the tendency to blame everything on the spouse: if he says, "I liked you because you seemed so understanding and tolerant," you can interrupt before he adds "but it turned out that you really weren't," and restate it to her, as "Your husband says you were tolerant and understanding—is that the way you saw yourself?" She may say, "Well, I wasn't always so understanding." If you can help her describe herself in more realistic terms without permitting him to exploit the opening, and if you do the same with him, you have helped each to begin looking at himself more objectively.

If one attacks the other in the course of this search for objectivity, I think you have to confront the attacker quite firmly with his exploitation of the situation, pointing out how it defeats their mutual goals. If you are lucky, he may respond to her comment, "Well, I wasn't always so understanding," with evidence that she really was, and each will support rather than attack the other. If one responds to the other's compliments about the past with the conventional modest disclaimer, the other naturally brings out evidence to support his complimentary position. Your goal is to have them arguing about each other's virtues rather than about each other's faults.

I think that your success in exploring and reducing the problems in marriage depends on your success in establishing a mutually supportive alliance between them. You first have to get them to sit down with you, however. You may not get a chance to work with both of them, because she inevitably will warn him, bluntly or subtly, that you are on her side, even if you have been very careful not to take sides when you have talked with her. The more she threatens him with your intervention, the less inclined he will be to come and see you.

CLERGYMAN 4: My church is strongly against drink, and as a result, I think that we get many women like this one. They feel so self-righteous when they make their husbands drive them to a church that thoroughly condemns drink. The husband knows the attitude of the church, so we speak whether we say anything or not.

DR. ALDRICH: Since people interpret the church not only in the way the representative of the church interprets it, but according to their own needs, I imagine that she sees the church accepting her and rejecting him, regardless of your attitude. She sets it up so that she can have this source of dependency and he can't, and the same may apply to the way in which she sets up the counseling sessions.

MR. HOWE: That may be one reason why he is not in the church. If the husbands of these women are so elusive, how about holding group sessions with the wives?

DR. ALDRICH: There have been reports of considerable success with group treatment of wives of alcoholics. Wives of alcoholics have a tendency to cry on one another's shoulders, however, and so encourage one another to project all of the problems onto the men. Groups of wives of alcoholics need strong leadership to avoid fostering an attitude of "We girls will have to take care of those poor weaklings."

CLERGYMAN 3: What about Alcoholics Anonymous?

DR. ALDRICH: It's great, when it works. Unfortunately, every alcoholic does not take to its approach, and some chapters have less effective programs than others. I think its effectiveness is primarily due to two factors: empathy and expectation. The alcoholic knows that the AA member has been through the same suffering and so is less inclined to see him as condescending or critical and more likely to trust his empathic response. Since the AA member gives evidence of success in overcoming his problem, it is easier for the alcoholic to incorporate an expectation of success into his own self-concept. I am sure that other factors contribute, but empathy and the atmosphere of expectation of success to me seem most significant.

CLERGYMAN 6: What about the man who doesn't take to AA but who wants to break the alcoholic habit? I have many problems like that in my parish ministry.

DR. ALDRICH: If he wants to break the habit, he has already taken the first step: acknowledging that he needs help. The next step is to build up confidence in his ability to control the impulse to drink. I think that the alcoholic deals with an underlying depression by drinking because he has responded to someone's expectation, early in his life, that he will be unable to control his drinking. He has responded by incorporating this expectation into his own self-image. Theoretically he should respond to the technique used to treat delinquent behavior, as in the case of Mr. Ellis' parishioner [Chapter Six]. After the control system is reinforced, his depression, or whatever that particular alcoholic is expressing through his impulse to drink, can be treated. I have to emphasize the theoretical in this discussion, because, in practice, psychiatrists have not been very successful in treating alcoholics.

MR. GRAY: My parishioner Gail doesn't seem to be a real alcoholic, and I don't think that treating her and her boyfriend as you suggested treating Helen and her husband would work out so well. How would you counsel her?

DR. ALDRICH: There are some differences in the approach to these two situations, although in both cases I would begin by looking for evidence of past strengths. In Gail's case, I might start by asking her about her marriage. She might say, "He was a wonderful guy, but I wasn't worthy of him and I couldn't live up to his standards." Such evidence of a past period of successful adjustment would encourage me. On the other hand, she might say, "That was even worse than the relationship I am in now," and I would have to go back to a point before the marriage to find a period of strength.

If her marriage had been at all good at one time, I would try to understand and to help her understand what happened to the successful adjustment and what led up to the subsequent affair. For the time being, I would avoid discussion of relatively recent events. She can better tolerate the anxiety that is stirred up when her current conflicts are explored if you have bolstered her confidence and self-esteem by focusing on some of the positive aspects of her life.

Meanwhile, however, Gail seems to have transferred dependency, anger, and attachment all to you. You cannot fulfill all her expectations and you will have to set some limits to her demands. At this point she can't trust anyone unless she can control him and she can't respect anyone she can control; this applies to you as well. I think you are wise to insist on seeing her in your office. Perhaps she calls you late at night in order to get an office appointment. She may feel, correctly or incorrectly, that she has to cause a commotion to get a ticket of admission to your office.

I think that the best way to help someone as dependent as Gail is to give her a half-hour office appointment once a week (or once every two weeks, or whatever I feel I can do) and restrict my attempts to help her to the office sessions. I would explain my plan carefully so that she would know what to expect. In this way I would guarantee her some continuity, and she wouldn't feel that she had to get her foot in the door by sounding a 4–11 alarm each time. At the end of the first session, I would look at my watch and say, "We can pick up on this when I see you next week (or in two weeks)." If she says it isn't enough, I'd say, "I'm sorry; this is what I think is appropriate for you." I have to be in charge. If she calls up the next night, I would say: "It is not going to be helpful to discuss this tonight. I'll see you in a week (or two weeks), less one day." When I limit her in this way, I am being firm, not cruel. I must set limits within which I will attempt to meet some but not all of her dependent needs. At the same time, by my attitude and interest in the successful part of her life, I am symbolically saying to her: "You've had the potential to make a satisfactory life, but something happened that led to your messing it up. If together we can understand what happened, maybe you can work out some way of returning."

You may find that Gail's "successful" past really wasn't so good, which would be discouraging. On the other hand, if she tells you it was a good marriage, you will want to know what sort of a person she married, what it was about her and about him that brought them together, and what happened to cause the trouble. Generally, if you can go back to the point where someone has made his best adjustment and find out what happened then, you encourage and support the patient's strengths; if you spend too much of your time checking out all the bad things, you emphasize his weaknesses and imply that there is not much to be done about him. The approach I am suggesting requires you to be somewhat directive. If you are nondirective with this sort of person, she goes over and over the same complaints, self-criticisms, and promises, and it doesn't help her. On the other hand, being somewhat directive and in charge of the treatment doesn't mean being in charge of the problem and giving all the answers.

MR. HOWE: Mr. Gray seems to have no trouble in ending his interviews with people like Gail, but I don't have the same success.

CLERGYMAN 8: The minister can't follow the same rigid schedule that the psychiatrist uses. It isn't so easy for us to terminate an interview. In order to end a conversation, we have to give the impression of being busy, of having other people waiting for us to see them.

CLERGYMAN 4: I set it up by scheduling my counseling in a series of interviews with several people in succession. I am afraid I lean on the fact that I am pressed for time and have other people waiting. In the long run this creates problems because someone who feels he needs to see me longer uses the excuse that I am pressed for time during my counseling hours in order to call me on the phone at other times.

DR. ALDRICH: By relying on outside pressure as your reason for not seeing them longer during the day, you indirectly encourage them to contact you at night.

CLERGYMAN 6: Many parishioners assume that they are the only ones you have to be concerned about. They believe their problems are unique.

DR. ALDRICH: Each person's problem seems more important to him than anybody else's. You can't convince him that it isn't by pointing out all the problems other people have.

Your position seems to be that they really need or deserve more time, which you would give them if you could. But the point that I want to make is that it is to the parishioner's advantage, as well as to yours, to set limits to the time you spend with him. When you imply, "I would give you more time if I had it," you suggest that he *should* have more time than you are giving him, and this position forces you to find reasons why you can't give it to him.

I think this issue needs resolution very early in your counseling. At the termination of the first interview you can say, "I would like to see you next week, and I will probably want to see you for a few weekly sessions, but I think we ought to keep them to half or three quarters of an hour each time." You can say it so that he understands you are structuring it this way not because that is all the time you can spare, but because that is what you think best for him. You are the person helping him and therefore you know more about it than he does. If you are convinced that what you are doing is in his best interests, he responds to the conviction behind your firmness.

CLERGYMAN 2: That's the clue word—"conviction." Most of the time I operate with a great deal of uncertainty.

DR. ALDRICH: You can be convinced that your decisions about counseling are in your parishioners' best interests without being certain that they are the best possible decisions. When you say, "We'll talk for half an hour," you may not know that precisely half an hour is exactly right for him, but you are more objective than he can be, and your judgment as to what he needs is better than his. He really thinks so, too, or he would not be coming to you for help; although you may sometimes feel uncertain, you're still in charge. Even if you feel that you should postpone making a definite plan until you've talked it over with a consultant, you should be the one in the meantime to determine the frequency and the duration of your counseling sessions.

When you consistently give a parishioner your full and undivided attention for the entire period you have promised him, and for that period only, he soon adjusts to it. For that period of time it is your most important job and at that time next week it will again be your most important job. This is reality, and to encourage him to expect otherwise is unrealistic and misleading. If he tells you about another pastor who sat up all night with a sick child, and asks if he isn't just as important, you can recognize his frustration but you should kindly and firmly stick to your guns. It will distract him from the goal of your interviews if he feels that he can manipulate you to give him more time. So when you say, "Half or three quarters of an hour is what I think is best for you," stick to it! It makes him feel more secure when he cannot manipulate you—he needs to feel that you know what you are doing. Once he realizes that you do know what you are doing, he stops bargaining for more time and gets down to business.

Even when he accepts your limits, however, he will probably want more time, and will find ways of trying to stretch out the time he has with you.

CLERGYMAN 2: When he gets ready to leave, he gets into the crux of what he wanted to talk about.

DR. ALDRICH: It is hard to cut somebody off when he is just about to give you the plum. But you have to say, "We'll talk about it next time." If you don't, you are in trouble, because he will learn, perhaps unconsciously, that the way to get more of your time is to delay anything important until the end of the interview. Solving his problem is a remote prospect, so the immediate gain of getting more of your time takes precedence. He therefore concentrates on beating around the bush until he sees that you are about ready to terminate, and then he gives you just enough to make you spend more time persuading him to give you the rest. In this way counseling can deteriorate into a contest for more of your time, which isn't going to cure him.

When you say, "We'll talk about it next time," he may tell you, "Next time may be different; I may not feel like talking about it." You reply, "Well, we'll see." You have to be firm.

MR. HOWE: I've tried to set limits, but I haven't been so firm as you suggest I should be. I think I now can, without feeling guilty that I am letting people down.

CLERGYMAN 6: Setting limits is the only thing I can do to keep any semblance of sanity. But I would like to ask what action the pastor should take to remind people who do not keep counseling appointments. Should we write them or phone them or what?

DR. ALDRICH: Unless I am worried about the possibility of suicide or some other emergency, I usually wait until a convenient time to call him up and say, "I missed you at our appointment today." He will probably then say, "Oh! I forgot all about it," and I say, "O.K., we'll make it next Wednesday." I don't make an issue of it unless it becomes a repetitive pattern. Then I say, "I think you have some mixed feelings about coming here, and maybe we ought to talk about them." I want to find out about his resistance to treatment, because I certainly can't treat him if he doesn't come. He may say, "I'm not sure that I should be seeing you about this problem." I would reply, "I realize that you have some doubts but I think that you should come in and talk them over with me." I imply that he owes it to me to clarify his feelings about our relationship.

Consistent lateness, like the delaying tactics, can represent an attempt to manipulate, and I try to interrupt the pattern before it gets established. A patient who has an hour's appointment and comes thirty minutes late for the first time may expect an hour's treatment. He gets thirty minutes. As I indicate that the time is up, he says, "You're not interrupting me now?" I don't say, "You would be inconveniencing the next person," because I don't want to put it off on someone else. I simply say, "Sorry, your hour was between ten and eleven." I imply that the hour is his, to be used in any way he wants. It is his privilege to come late, and I am not going to get angry, but I am also not going to reward him by giving him extra time.

I am referring now to the chronically late person. It is a different matter if there is a blizzard, and the car got stuck. In the isolated instance you use your judgment. I am sure it is more difficult for you than for me to keep to a schedule. A lot depends on your priorities: I imagine that you get to your services on time but that your hospital calls may be more irregular. But I think scheduling is important for counseling.

CLERGYMAN 6: But this approach seems to conflict with my obligation to the parishioner and his concern for me as a so-called friend. When an emotional individual calls up in the middle of the night, sobbing and apologizing for calling and saying: "But, Pastor, I just have to talk to you. I can't stand this any longer alone here. Please listen to me," what do I do? How far should I go in listening to him at that particular time? Is it reasonable, when he is upset like this, to say: "Look. You'd better go back to bed now. It's late; you need sleep and I need sleep."

DR. ALDRICH: A lot depends on what has gone before in your relationship with this particular parishioner. If you have not established a counseling relationship with him, I would treat the call as a cry for help that requires an immediate response. If you have established a counseling relationship, you face the same kind of dilemma as the doctor whose neurotic patient complains of a pain in the abdomen in the middle of the night. He may have to check to make sure it is not appendicitis; you may have to listen for a while until you understand what's happening. If it's really a new crisis, you need to know how long it has been going on, what precipitated it, and why he is so concerned about it right now. This information, on top of the information you already have about him, gives you the basis for deciding whether to continue your attempts to help him at that time, or to postpone them until a regular or an extra appointment.

However, if it is simply a restatement of a long-standing complaint, I would be quite firm. I would not tell him to go back to sleep but would say: "The time to talk about it is at our regular appointment. I know it is difficult, but I am sure you can tolerate it and we will talk about it when I see you next time." If there is anything about the pattern that is unusual, I treat it as an emergency until I find otherwise.

CLERGYMAN 4: I agree that setting limits is appropriate, if you have had a number of interviews with him and he has called a number of times on the phone. But once I said to one of my parishioners, "All right. I understand how you feel, but I think we should talk about it when I see you next Thursday," and I haven't seen her or heard from her since. She neither calls nor comes to the office, and she and her children have stopped coming to church. She felt rejected and she made the children feel rejected. I feel that I have missed the boat somewhere.

DR. ALDRICH: No, I don't think you've missed the boat, at least not on the basis of what you have communicated to us. I think she tried, unconsciously, to trap you through your concern about protecting the children. But you cannot protect the children by meeting this kind of demand; in fact, if you let her use them to enforce her demands on this occasion, she will use them even more for this kind of blackmail. If she could get her way by having headaches, she would have more headaches—not consciously contrived, but headaches just the same. If she gets her way by manipulating the children, she'll manipulate them even more.

Early in a relationship, as soon as I see this pattern forming, I make it quite clear that I understand she gets upset and perhaps lonely in the evening, but that I cannot undertake to respond to her at night except in emergencies, and that I will be the one to decide what constitutes an emergency. I point out to her that one of the goals of counseling is to help her cope with her problems; to build a pattern of relying on me will defeat this purpose. In other words, I give her fair warning. The longer it goes on, the harder it is to reverse, but if you catch it early in the game, she will soon understand that it is not in her best interest to attempt to resolve these problems on the telephone or at night.

If she has left you for this reason, she has left because she is looking for another pastor whom she can manipulate more easily. The fact that your lack of response to her manipulation has made her go somewhere else doesn't mean that you would have solved the problem by responding. You would only have perpetuated it, and it would eventually have come to the same end; the more you responded, the greater would become her expectations, and at some point you could no longer respond. To carry out appropriate counseling you have to take some risks, and one is the risk of losing your patient or parishioner. That's why you have to believe in what you are doing; if you don't believe that your procedure is in his best interests, you hesitate or compromise at the wrong time. Keep in mind, too, that you just can't help some people no matter what you do. It is a tragedy to see how they make themselves and their families miserable, but the fact that it is a tragedy doesn't mean that any of us are omnipotent enough to change them. In her case, I think you have done the right thing. In the long run, after she finds that her way does not produce results, she may come back; if she does, you have a better start with her.

She is like a patient with appendicitis who wants treatment but refuses surgery. The doctor has to say: "I must treat you the way I believe you need to be treated or I can't treat you. I can't let you decide how you are going to be treated." The same reasoning applies to the patient or parishioner with an emotional problem. You can't let him prescribe how he is going to be treated. You have to stick to your decision and risk losing him. Otherwise, he will take up time that you could be devoting to people who can respond. You can't afford to let a person use time to no avail, because your time is too valuable.

CHAPLAIN NIGHSWONGER: The pastor's situation is somewhat different, however, because people expect us to maintain our constituency. They don't insist that we help anybody, but the pastor is under a lot of pressure not to lose parishioners.

CLERGYMAN 4: You see, Dr. Aldrich, our counseling experiences spill back into the church family. The youth groups are affected when someone's youngsters don't show up. Everyone knows that in that family things have started to erupt again. The young people in the group become upset, and the effect spreads.

DR. ALDRICH: I grant you it can be a tough situation, but you will not avoid it by trying to meet her demands, because the demands will multiply faster than you can meet them. You will not help her with her emotional problem by responding on her terms; all you will do is get yourself further entangled. But all of us have to make compromises.

CLERGYMAN 4: I guess the problem is how to take care of my own frustrations when I run into something I don't know how to handle.

DR. ALDRICH: I expect it is more frustrating to you than it would be to me because it so clearly affects the rest of your work. But are you sure that you aren't magnifying the effect this woman's defection will have on your congregation because you feel that somehow you have failed her? Your feeling of inadequacy with her may contribute to your fear that this one family will wreck the congregation.

CLERGYMAN 8: Perhaps a pastoral call would help. We are supposed to go to our people; they don't always come to us.

DR. ALDRICH: It might be the only way to reestablish communication. In this kind of situation and for a few others, as in the case of a "housebound" woman who is afraid of going out, the pastoral call may be combined with a limited approach to counseling. Generally, however, I think counseling should be kept in your offices, where it is easier to separate counseling from social visits, and interruptions can be better controlled— at least you're responsible if they're not. It is also harder to set time limits to a home visit.

CLERGYMAN 7: A woman can create problems for the pastor who makes house calls if she begins to see in him a substitute for her husband. He can have trouble even if his response to her overtures is completely professional.

DR. ALDRICH: Even if she doesn't make overtures, he can find himself accused of misbehavior, if the difference between fact and wish-fulfillment fantasy isn't too clear to her. This confusion is not uncommon and explains why the doctor always has a nurse in the room when he examines the undressed female patient. It is not because he fears that something might actually happen, but because the strength of the patient's fantasies may obscure the accuracy of her perception.

However, if you are aware of the possibility and don't close your eyes to signs of seductiveness, you usually can deal with it without making her feel guilty. You also must be aware of your own feelings, so that you don't give her encouragement without realizing it.

CLERGYMAN 4: We are, or should be, always careful not to talk about intimate problems on a pastoral call. The call is always made in daytime when the children are there.

CLERGYMAN 2: I reverse the usual procedure. I only make pastoral calls by invitation, but I have an office period during which parishioners can see me without appointment. I wonder, from the pastor's point of view, whether I am shirking my pastoral duty when I don't make routine pastoral house calls.

I do make calls with the sick, but I spend many hours a day in the office.

DR. ALDRICH: Your procedure is more efficient, since you can spend more time seeing people instead of traveling. I suppose that if you have a large number of parishioners, you cannot afford to spend much time in travel. On the other hand, if your appointments are always by request, the squeaking wheel gets the grease; people who are more diffident and who hesitate to ask may need you more than some of the more aggressive people.

Considering the numbers who might benefit from counseling, however, you may have to make some kind of selection. In each case your decision about setting up a formal counseling arrangement will depend on a combination of factors: the number of parishioners who need counseling; the kinds of problems they present and your appraisal of your own capacities to provide help; the availability of alternative resources—psychiatrists, clinics, social agencies—in your community; your church's policy about the relative importance of counseling in your pastoral work; and a number of other personal and organizational considerations. All these factors plus another set of factors related to the parishioner's and his family's specific characteristics are relevant to the pastor's planning in any specific situation.

Chapter Nine

THE
PSYCHIATRIC
CONSULTANT

Ian's and John's problems at first appear to be very similar. Differences emerge as the cases are discussed in greater detail, and the pastor's need for assistance in clarifying the nature and severity of their problems is demonstrated. The wide variety of ways in which the clergyman can use psychiatric consultation is emphasized, along with the range of his potential resources in the community.

MR. IVES: Ian is thirty years old, married, with three young children. He has a college degree and works as a certified public accountant. He has been active in the church and has held various positions of leadership. From all appearances he was an exceptionally stable and capable person.

One day about nine months ago, he entered my office with all the signs of depression. He said, "This may come as a shock to you, but things are not right between my wife and me." They had not had intercourse for quite some time, and he felt he was not sexually adequate. He believed that his wife wanted more of a man than he was and that he was not able to give her the masculine support she needed.

In a later interview he told me of his suspicion that his wife was having a flirtation with the man across the street. He denied that it made him angry, saying he felt rather depressed that she had to turn to someone else. He hesitated to say anything to his wife or the other man or to anybody else.

He then told me that he feared that he would act like his father who was an alcoholic. He described his mother as a stable person, quiet but, nonetheless, the dominant person in his life. She nagged at his father, who responded by going out to the corner pub to forget about her. He saw his father as weak, and after several sessions he told me that he actually hated his father. He also hated to see the image of his father cropping up in himself.

Ian has a younger brother who apparently got along well with the father. His dad would take the brother fishing, and Ian would stay home, feel hostile, and then turn to his mother. Perhaps that is why at a fairly early age he turned away from what he felt were masculine expressions toward more abstract thinking.

One of the problems he had been having with intercourse was premature ejaculation; he had turned to masturbation, hoping that it would help, but it made him feel guilty. He said that his wife excited him too much; he felt like a boy with a woman for the first time, who got so excited that he couldn't live up to her expectations. Ian speaks more freely than most people about sexual matters. He told me that during intercourse he could never think of his wife as a person, but instead thought only of female genitals.

He said that his family needed him, and that he was only enduring life to supply what they needed. He was not living creatively, but only going through the motions. Although his marital problems made him depressed, I had the feeling that he derived almost a masochistic feeling of enjoyment from his miserable situation.

DR. ALDRICH: Have you seen the wife?

MR. IVES: Yes, a couple of months after he first saw me, he asked me to drop in to see his wife, Irene, because she was feeling depressed. When I called on her, she was emotionally keyed up. She seemed depressed, but said depression was not her problem, although she didn't really say what her problem was. She seemed to behave inconsistently, reacting at times like a sophisticated woman and at other times giggling like a little girl.

I couldn't get anywhere, so I asked her to drop by my office. When she got there she seemed less flighty, and said she was particularly depressed in the mornings, and it was getting worse. I suggested some psychiatric help.

DR. ALDRICH: Did she seem more depressed than Ian?

MR. IVES: No, she didn't, but she said she was much more depressed in the morning, and this was in the afternoon.

A few days later Ian telephoned, and said that Irene was in hysterics. She had just admitted to him that she had been having an affair with the man across the street. When I arrived, she was in the midst of the hysterics, but her basic feeling was guilt. She kept asking: "Will God forgive me for this? How can he possibly accept me now?" Eventually she quieted down, and we made another appointment.

When I saw her later in my office, she said that she had not become what she considered an adequate woman, and she had been searching for someone who could make her "feel loved and needed, and feel that she was a woman." In talking this over, she constantly alluded to her father, to his expectations for her and his involvement in her life, and particularly to his feelings about her when she became pregnant with the first child. At that time he was very hostile, and she didn't understand why. Her father is a self-educated man who has been an athlete and is fairly successful in a small business.

DR. ALDRICH: Ian is still tied to his mother, and Irene is still tied to her father, so it isn't surprising that the two of them have sexual problems as well as other problems in their marriage.

MR. IVES: There is considerable difference in their backgrounds. He has a college degree and she only finished high school. Although she is not unintelligent, she often says that Ian is "way above her." She likes to go to parties and have a good time, whereas he likes to sit around and read or talk.

The man across the street is the opposite of Ian. He is a telephone lineman who is often home during the day. Irene thinks his work is very masculine, and when he is with her she feels like a real woman.

DR. ALDRICH: This case illustrates the consequences of failure to resolve the problems of the developmental stage of family relationships. Ian perceived his father as inadequate and his mother as strong. His father siphoned off the brother, leaving Ian close to his mother; perhaps he became her confidant with whom she could discuss the father's deficiencies. The tie between mother and son was maintained past the point of its usual resolution, and so, keeping mother in first place in his affections, he married a woman who has less education and, I feel sure, is depreciated in other ways. I suspect that the only kind of sexual relationship he *can* have is with a depreciated woman, but even his wife isn't depreciated enough for him really to be sexually adequate.

Ian is relatively scientific and unemotional about the sexual information he gives you, consistent with a need to detach the sexual side of woman from the woman as a person, as he does in the intercourse fantasy. Even though he sided with mother, he may have perceived father as the weaker victim of mother's domination. As a male, he is afraid that the same thing will happen to him, and so he tries to find a wife who won't threaten him. But although Irene is intellectually inferior, she is still a woman. Premature ejaculation is usually a response to a woman who is perceived as dangerous to men, particularly in the sexual or most intimate relationship. Ian is not so frightened that he becomes impotent, but his premature ejaculation suggests that he is in a hurry to get away, to retire to a position of safety. At the same time he is depressed because he has not had a satisfactory sexual relationship with his wife; on a conscious level he wants to be adequate as a man.

Ian's fear of his wife is compounded if she looks for another man. But his subtle depreciation of her interest in casual conversation and less intellectual pursuits intensifies her feeling of inadequacy about her education; to bolster her ego, she starts to visit her neighbor. The telephone lineman meets her immediate needs, but the relationship also produces guilt and depression.

Irene's conscious guilt concerns her adultery; Ian's concerns masturbation. Guilt about masturbation is not always about masturbation itself; it may have more to do with the fantasies occurring during masturbation. Their nature in Ian's case is not clear, but they may well resemble the intercourse fantasies, and his masturbation guilt may indirectly be affected by guilt related to his feelings about his mother. He has covered up his conflict about sex, mother, and masculinity to some extent; he's married and has a family and has an outlet in his work. When his wife began to look for someone else, however, the protective balance was upset, his inner conflict threatened to emerge, and his symptoms appeared.

The fact, if indeed a fact, that Irene's father was furious with her for her legitimate pregnancy suggests that he continues to be strongly involved with her. On her part, this continuing tie may to some extent account for her marrying a highly intellectual man who is quite different from her father. Her unconscious guilt about the implications of the tie encouraged her choice of a husband who depreciates, or punishes, her. Her guilt may also account for her making her relationship with the other man obvious to Ian. Thus, both Ian and Irene have looked for a marriage partner who fills their particular needs. They use each other to defend themselves against the emergence of earlier conflicts, and in that way form an informal and

somewhat shaky defensive alliance. The alliance survives some
of the sexual problems, but breaks down when the other man
enters the scene.

With the breakdown of their defensive alliance, they each
resume the effort to work out unresolved problems of earlier
life. They are both depressed because unconsciously they feel
so guilty about the implications of their parental ties. Their
unconscious guilt is added to their conscious guilt about adultery and masturbation.

When Ian talked with you, he made several references to his
avoidance of traditional masculine expression. This suggests a
possibility in his background we have not discussed: hidden or
latent homosexuality. Homosexuality, either in hidden or in
evident form, is one way of resolving the sexual conflict of a
boy's prolonged and intense attachment to his mother. If the
man's sexual object is another man, the question of a sexual
component in his tie to his mother seems academic.

Homosexuality is a difficult problem to treat, even by trained
psychiatrists, and there is no advantage to bringing it out in the
open if it is hidden. That makes it difficult to test—how do we
know whether it's there unless we explore it—but I would
rather not know than open up a Pandora's box. I wouldn't avoid
it, however, if Ian brought up the subject; if he did say that he
had been troubled by homosexual thoughts or impulses, I
would not panic. Since he undoubtedly would be ashamed of
it, I would be careful not to let him think that I rejected him
because of it. I would listen for a while, and if he asked what
could be done about it, I would suggest that a psychiatrist
could give him better advice, and help him find a psychiatrist
who was interested in treating this kind of problem.

When Ian talked about his wife's flirtation, I wondered if he
was signaling the beginning of a paranoid psychosis. One of
the common ideas of persecution that characterizes the paranoid patient is the conviction that his wife is unfaithful. Freud
believed that the basis of the paranoid psychosis was an un-

acceptable homosexual impulse that the patient projected onto others so that he could say, in effect, "I am not homosexual; it is those people out there who, in one way or another, are making homosexual overtures to me." Sometimes the homosexual implication is obvious; more often it is disguised, as "They are laughing at me because my wife is cheating on me," implying that he is not capable of satisfying her sexually, which in turn implies that he is effeminate.

However, as you told us more about him, Ian seemed more depressed and less paranoid, and as you went farther into the story, it began to appear that Irene's affair was realistic and not a delusion. As this example suggests, case formulation must always be subject to modification as you learn more about the individual.

CLERGYMAN 5: I'm not sure that we have satisfactorily dealt with Irene's relationship to the church. When Mr. Ives saw her in hysterics, she kept saying, "Will God forgive me?" How do you think we should deal with that?

DR. ALDRICH: I think there are two meanings to that question. One meaning has to do with God's forgiveness, and it would be presumptuous for me to attempt to respond. In my practice I would refer that kind of question to whichever one of you was appropriate. The other meaning, however, has more to do with herself. "Will God forgive me?" also means "Am I forgivable?"; she is asking you, or her husband, or whoever is there. She seeks forgiveness because she feels guilty and ashamed. I would not withhold forgiveness, but I also would not be in too much of a hurry to volunteer it until I knew what I really was forgiving. If her affair was in response to a depression due to guilt, premature reassurance might close off your avenue to helping with her depression.

I am not sure that we know what upset the balance of this marriage and precipitated the breakdown. It may have been simply the availability during the day of the man across the street. Or it may have been something that as yet is not clear. It would be important to understand the precipitating factors before trying to predict the course of treatment or their response to it. A favorable sign is the fact that both are asking for help. I would anticipate that individual psychiatric treatment of each partner would take longer than marital counseling and would cost more; the wear and tear on the marriage as each wrestled with the resolution of earlier relationships would be considerable. On the other hand, the results, if successful, might be more lasting or less vulnerable to stress. The goal of marital counseling would be to try to reconstruct the earlier defenses that made it possible to adapt. If the couple decided on marital counseling, you might consider referral to a family agency.

CLERGYMAN 1: How do you feel about referrals to counseling agencies when there apparently is a psychiatric problem?

DR. ALDRICH: It depends on the agency. I think that one of the clergyman's jobs is to know the resources in his community—not simply their addresses, but the quality of their services and the ease with which you can make referrals. It helps to know who in the community is particularly interested in older people, for instance, or in alcoholics or in adolescents. It also helps to know which agencies have long waiting lists and which can step in in a crisis. The same kind of information about the psychiatrists in the community is useful.

There are several aspects of Ian's and Irene's problem that I think should be clarified before a pastor should take on the responsibility of counseling them. If it turns out that she is not severely depressed, that he is neither psychotic nor wrestling with a homosexual problem that is too close to the surface, and that there have been enough past strengths in the marriage to provide some encouragement for marital counseling, the pastor might well undertake the task, preferably with the couple as a unit.

MR. JONES: I have a case that I don't know how to manage, and maybe it falls in the same category. John is a commercial artist about forty-five years of age. He is married, with a son age fifteen and a daughter age twelve. He works now for a small advertising agency. He has had several jobs but has never had one with much responsibility, although he holds a rather responsible position in our church and used to teach Sunday school. He came to me quite dramatically one evening and said that he wanted to resign his position in the church. He and his wife Judy had not been getting along well; he was going to divorce her and then do away with himself.

Fortunately, I had been warned earlier of his depression and suicidal plan by a friend of his, who works with him. I had only been in the parish about three months when he told me about John. I called the neighboring minister and got some recommendations about resources in the community. Meanwhile the friend had advised John to talk with me before he did anything drastic.

I was somewhat prepared, therefore, when he came in to resign. I talked with him for a while about his depression and his marital difficulties, and then recommended a marriage counselor. He didn't think that his wife would be interested, but I offered to call her and see. Although she was quite reluctant at first, she finally agreed to see the marriage counselor.

They worked with the marriage counselor for about eight months, and things seemed to be going along fairly well. But about a month ago, Judy called me for an appointment. She is a journalist and a rather dominating type of individual. She said that John had told her that he could no longer carry on and that she should commit him to the state hospital. She said they had stopped seeing the marriage counselor when he asked them to bring their children in for a consultation; they thought the children were too young to be involved.

I asked if he had seen his family doctor, but he doesn't have one. I then told Judy that I would try to get John an appointment with a psychiatric outpatient clinic. I called the clinic, but they said they preferred to have him call in for the appointment. He did so, but when he learned how much it was going to cost, he said they couldn't afford it. This isn't realistic because they are both working and have two incomes; Judy told me that they are several years ahead on their mortgage payments.

DR. ALDRICH: Finances can be a realistic deterrent to treatment, but they can also be used as a rationalization for not getting treatment. Some depressed patients feel that they are not worth spending money on, regardless of the amount.

John has told at least two people that he plans to commit suicide. You might think that if somebody really wanted to commit suicide, he would go ahead and do it without telling anyone. But most suicidal patients don't want only to die; they also want to live, but they don't believe they can cope by themselves. The communication of a suicidal intention is the equivalent of a call for help. John tells his friend, "I am going to commit suicide." The friend talks to you and persuades John to see you, and you refer him to a source of treatment. This doesn't mean that he uses the threat simply to get attention. Until proven otherwise, you have to assume that the threat is a sign of desperation. The great majority of people who make suicide attempts call for help before the attempt by telling somebody in one way or another about their plans. There used to be a widespread belief that people who talk about suicide won't do it. It couldn't be more wrong!

I wonder how you felt about the suicide threat. How seriously did you take it? Your referral to the marriage counselor surprised me a little—I expected that you would have thought first of a psychiatrist who has the opportunity for hospital treatment. I am also surprised that the counselor wasn't more concerned.

MR. JONES: I told the counselor about the suicide threat, but I was swayed by John's emphasis on the marriage difficulty.

DR. ALDRICH: You thought that he was using the threat as a lever to manipulate his environment?

MR. JONES: That's right. He had also mentioned that he thought he should pack up his clothes and stay at the Y.M.C.A. for a while.

DR. ALDRICH: He also said that he wanted to be committed. What does commitment mean to him? To a layman uninformed of recent changes in psychiatry, commitment often means old-fashioned barred windows and the "snake pit," which a person would want to avoid if at all possible, unless he believed he deserved punishment. Commitment may also mean regression to a totally dependent and passive adaptation, in which he can avoid any active involvement. Another possible basis for seeking commitment is a need for protection against his hostile impulses. When somebody says, "They ought to lock me up," he usually implies "before I do harm to myself or to someone else." He may be having a great deal of trouble with his anger —either turning it inward as in the suicide threat, or fearing that it will break out and lead him to hurt somebody. Most of John's suggested "solutions"—suicide, divorce, the Y, commitment—remove him from the environment of his wife, and from the possibly dangerous consequences of their interaction. When the counselor or the clinic offers him the chance to look more closely at his feelings, he is apprehensive. At this point he may be asking not for treatment, but for protection. He may be asking for help in controlling his feelings, rather than in stirring them up. He sounds to me like a frightened man.

Does he have any feeling of persecution, a feeling that, somehow or other, people are all against him? It's a matter of degree; most of us project responsibility for our troubles to some extent, but the paranoid person accentuates this tendency to the point of belief in an organized plot.

MR. JONES: John quit his previous job because he felt he had been cheated out of a promotion. He gave me the impression that he had not been treated fairly, but I did not see evidence of a belief in an organized plot.

His wife said that the doctor who delivered the children told her, "Don't ever burden your husband with these children." He gets quite upset about the children, and doesn't want them around. Even now they have to go to their rooms if he comes home with work to do.

DR. ALDRICH: He taught Sunday school and yet he can't stand his children. That sounds paradoxical, but it is usually easier to be objective with other people's children than with one's own. He may be jealous of their claim to a dependent relationship with his wife. That's not too uncommon, and can be intense in parents, usually fathers, who have many residual dependent needs.

I wonder if this man's age is contributing to his depression. In his twenties, he could rationalize taking subordinate jobs for the time being, thinking that in the future he would become an executive. But when he has been passed over at forty, and realizes that he is not going to fulfill his fantasies of success, it is harder for him to deny his feelings of passivity and he becomes more depressed.

The counselor may not have been concerned about the suicide risk because John may have denied it. By the time he gets to the clinic or hospital or psychiatrist, the person who seemed desperate when he asked you for a referral may have been able to cover up. By arranging a referral, you have taken the edge off his desperation; his urgency decreases to a point at which the relationship necessary to permit him to talk about his feelings may be more of a threat than the feelings themselves. He says, "I need help," but once he gets to the source of help, he is more scared of help than of getting along without it. So he talks about superficialities and the psychiatrist or counselor does not perceive him as suicidal.

MR. JONES: He admits that he is afraid to expose his weaknesses. He says that there are some things that he can't bear to have people know.

How seriously should I take this problem? I have opened the door on a couple of occasions to try to help both of them. John now says that he is going to look into another clinic he has heard about.

DR. ALDRICH: There is some evidence that he is frightened of his own potential to hurt himself and he may be looking for somebody who will be quite firm with him. He may need someone to say: "Look, this trouble has reached the point where you need professional help that I simply can't give you. I know it is difficult to talk about it and you are scared, but the time has come when you must." If he then says, "Oh, no, I'll be all right," you say firmly: "I am sorry. This has gone far enough so that you are not in a position to know what's best for you."

The success of this approach depends on your relationship with him and to some extent on your ability to make a firm recommendation without appearing to reject him or to wish to "unload" him. I don't think he will carry it through unless he sees you are convinced he needs that kind of help. You need to let a person know when you do not consider his problem within your area of competence and then stick to this decision; otherwise, he uses you as a protection against involvement with his therapist. He returns to you to be bailed out or to start over when the going gets rough. If he does return, it is almost always better for him if you make clear your belief that he should talk over his doubts and questions with his therapist.

In John's case you might say, "Look, I think you should let

me talk frankly with the marital counselor or the psychiatrist at the hospital about the conversations I've had with you." Since he has spoken with you confidentially, you need his permission to tell the therapist what has been going on. I am worried about this man.

CLERGYMAN 8: You are saying that this man is really sick—he is not just facing a difficult problem that he can't cope with at the moment?

DR. ALDRICH: There's not a clear distinction between being really sick and having a problem, but rather a continuum ranging from the hypothetical person who is problem free to the person who needs hospital treatment and protection so badly that involuntary care is necessary. Furthermore, people don't stay put at one point on the continuum—they get better or worse without notice.

The lack of a clear-cut distinction between the "sickness" and the "problem" makes it difficult to decide whether to refer or to keep on working with someone. You often have to live with uncertainty. Even when you're convinced that referral is appropriate, you may have to ride along with the situation for a while. Some people almost have to get worse before they can accept help. This is particularly true of the paranoid person with ideas of persecution, often backed up by voices, who is convinced that people are against him. Logical argument doesn't help because such people are completely convinced that other people are the sources of the voices they hear and that other people are actually persecuting them. They usually reject any kind of treatment, although if you can manage neither to agree with them nor to argue with them but simply to let them know that you perceive their problem as a psychiatric condition, they eventually may agree to a diagnostic exploration. It may require a number of return visits, however, going over the same material each time.

CLERGYMAN 1: How about commitment?

DR. ALDRICH: Commitment may sometimes be necessary, particularly if the person is dangerous to himself or others. But commitment is a drastic step for family members to initiate. They are afraid of his later resentment. If he has the delusion that his wife is running around, he interprets any move toward hospitalization as a means of getting him out of the way, so that she can go on with her affair. Sometimes the family needs a great deal of the clergyman's support when commitment is unavoidable.

However, I don't think it is a good idea for an outsider to sign commitment papers. The family members often don't want to sign; they say, "He will never forgive us," and they may be right. But you can't take this kind of responsibility for people in your parish. The family has the responsibility, and I guess they are stuck with it.

CLERGYMAN 5: Last week a boy of twenty, an only child, told me that he was contemplating not only suicide but also killing his mother and father. I made an immediate referral to a psychiatrist, but I was frightened.

DR. ALDRICH: Tragedies of this kind occasionally do occur. However, it is reassuring as well as frightening to hear about it in advance. If killing his parents and himself is his only objective, telling you about it diminishes the chances of his doing it. I believe that he told you because he wants somebody to stop him. He was signaling for help, and he put his message in terms you couldn't miss. I think that if someone told me that he planned to kill mother, father, and himself, I would say, "I can see that you are terribly frightened by these feelings." He would agree, and I would say, "You are telling me about them because you are looking for help to do something about them, aren't you?" "Yes." "O.K., you came to the right place. I will help you." I would then go on to ask him how long he's felt this way, and what he has tried to do about it and about his increasing desperation; and in other ways I would try to demonstrate my understanding that he is asking for help *not* to kill. Sending him to the hospital, or making a referral, or whatever I have to do becomes easier when he senses my empathy.

CLERGYMAN 6: It has been helpful to see the importance of talking with the psychiatrist or the doctor about people who come to my attention. My tendency heretofore has been to unload the individual on the doctor and expect that he will be taken care of without too much further work on my part. We seem to need more communication.

DR. ALDRICH: Some of the psychiatrist's reluctance to consult with clergymen stems from his concern that he may become the recipient of all your problems. He will hesitate to volunteer if he feels that he will be obliged to take over. Most psychotherapists do not take on more patients than they feel they can treat appropriately, and their schedules are often full.

It is easier if you know a psychiatrist with whom you are free to share informally the things you are worried about, recognizing that he has only a limited time available. Almost all psychotherapists work on a fixed time basis and do not feel it is fair to the patient to permit interruptions. When I telephone another psychiatrist, I usually say to the secretary, "This is Dr. Aldrich; is Dr. Blank with a patient?" Usually the answer is yes, so I say, "Could you tell me when it would be convenient to call?" or "Could you ask him to call me as soon as he breaks, as it is something of an emergency?" Once the psychiatrist understands that you recognize his problems, he is more inclined to help you with your problems.

CLERGYMAN 8: Suppose I have a parishioner whom I have nurtured along to the point where he accepts the idea of psychiatric help. I then call Dr. Aldrich and say, "I have a parishioner who I think is now ready for psychiatric care." Unfortunately, Dr. Aldrich is snowed under and can't take on my parishioner. What do I do under the circumstances? Do I call another psychiatrist? It has taken six months or a year to get this person to this point. Who knows if he will still be ready a week, a month, or six months from now, when you are ready to take him?

DR. ALDRICH: The search for psychiatric assistance can be very frustrating, particularly when the need is for psychotherapy. It is usually less difficult to get a patient into a hospital, or to find a psychiatrist for outpatient treatment by medication.

However, if it has taken six months for you to get this man ready, and the readiness is so fragile that he cannot brook delay, the pathway from your office to my office is going to be rocky no matter how soon I have an opening. If his motivation is so tenuous that it can't survive a period of waiting, the chances are that the therapy won't take anyway. After six months of urging the person may be sick of being persuaded, so he finally says: "All right, all right, I'll go. Get off my back, I'll go." He then comes to me only to prove to you, the person on whom he is really dependent, that psychiatry won't work. I can't do much about that.

On the other hand, it would be much better for all concerned if more psychotherapeutic care were available so that it would not be so difficult to find.

CHAPLAIN NIGHSWONGER: Doesn't the success of a referral depend on the capability of the psychiatrist as well as on the capability of the minister?

DR. ALDRICH: Certainly, and I don't mean to exculpate psychiatrists who are unperceptive or rude or maladroit. You need to pick your man. However, a study in New York City showed that preparation for the referral was a more important factor in predicting the success of psychotherapy than the experience or professional discipline of the therapist. If a patient comes to me saying to himself, "I'm only here to satisfy my pastor, and I am going to prove to him that I don't need to be here," neither I nor any psychiatrist I know is skillful enough to be successful in more than a minority of cases.

A disadvantage of referral is that it provides the client with time to reflect and to build up resistance to doing anything about his problem. One reason why I believe it is so important for pastors to be comfortable in a counseling relationship is that they are often in the most strategic position to accomplish something. The parishioner has told you about his problem because he trusts you to be understanding; his trust is not easily transferred to the unknown psychiatrist or other psychotherapist, no matter how carefully the referral is made. Even after six months your parishioner may not be ready to move outside your orbit or to transfer his allegiance.

It might solve some of the difficulties if you knew a psychiatrist with whom you could consult about your parishioner during the six months. There is a type of consultation between professionals about a patient which does not require the patient to visit the psychiatrist. The clergyman, the general practitioner, the school counselor, sometimes the public health nurse, occasionally the social worker in the welfare department —these are all people who are on the firing line, and are more likely than the psychiatrist to be the first port of call for people with troubles. Consultation can help them carry on their own work.

The consultation can be set up as a formal teaching session, with individuals taking turns to present cases to a group such as ours that meets at regular intervals. On the other hand, consultation can be much more informal, as when Chaplain Nighswonger calls me and explains a situation. I may say, "Perhaps I should see your parishioner once or twice for a diagnostic appraisal," making it clear that the parishioner is still his client.

His client may accept a diagnostic consultation with me more readily than he would accept a transfer of full responsibility.

Alternatively, I may say to Chaplain Nighswonger, "It sounds as if you are doing all right—go ahead"; or I may have a suggestion. Although I cannot take responsibility for a patient I do not interview, I can relieve his mind on specific points. That should give him more confidence in his counseling, and he will become more helpful to his parishioner.

CHAPLAIN NIGHSWONGER: When a pastor can find a colleague in psychiatry with whom he can communicate and consult, he can apply what he learns in one consultation to other parishioners with similar problems. Even if the psychiatrist is overburdened, he should be interested in what we are doing, because we are actually helping him by taking on a case load rather than referring more to him. So he should be glad to help.

DR. ALDRICH: He certainly should, but I am afraid that not all of us respond as we should. Some psychiatrists don't like to consult with members of other professions; some are afraid that encouraging others to treat emotional problems will cut in on their practices; some believe that their religious views differ so much from the pastor's that they would never be able to understand one another. I am not sure that the last two objections are justified, but the first has some validity. The role of a consultant is quite different from the role of a psychotherapist, and it doesn't suit all psychiatrists.

If an interested psychiatrist is not available, it should be possible to work out a consultative relationship with someone in a family agency. A social worker can often be helpful in consultation with the clergyman.

CLERGYMAN 6: A man called up this week to ask to see me. He is now thirty-five years old. He was diagnosed schizophrenic when he was in his teens. He spent a year in a veterans hospital, and has been committed once since then, but he didn't stay because his family got him out. He is divorced, but there is a continual problem between him, his ex-wife, and his family. I told him frankly: "I really don't know how much I can do for you. I am a minister, not a psychiatrist. If I can help you on this basis, I want to do so." But I wonder how much I can do for him.

DR. ALDRICH: I think you may be able to help keep him stabilized, if your goals are not too ambitious. If his illness were an acute one of short duration, you would have to be much more careful. It's safer when the illness has gone on for years. Chronic patients can often be maintained outside hospitals by occasional brief periods of talking with an understanding listener who doesn't try to make dramatic changes. It is sometimes hard to avoid the temptation to inquire further into all the unrealistic aspects, but your interventions should be determined by your perception of what is realistic. You listen to the unrealistic material, but without much response until he begins to talk about more realistic concerns. You may have to interrupt an unrealistic monologue with "How are things going at work?" or "How are things going with your hobby in the basement shop?" If he tells you about that kind of activity, you prick up your ears and encourage him to tell you more. Your interest in the reality-oriented part of him encourages his interest.

The last few cases we have discussed seem more severe, and probably should be referred to a psychiatrist or to another mental health professional. Although the clergyman may not be counseling directly with them, he nevertheless can be important to the success of treatment: first, in the way he makes the referral and helps his parishioner make the transition to the treatment agent; second, in remaining available in the usual pastoral role for support and encouragement to both patient and family during treatment; and third, in his readiness to resume a counseling role after formal treatment has been completed.

Cases of this type represent a minority in the pastor's counseling ministry. For the majority of the parishioners who seek his counsel, the clergyman is the primary if not the only professional source of help. As the seminars have shown, these parishioners provide him not only with a challenge but with an opportunity to contribute substantially to the well-being of his congregation.

EPILOGUE

The clergyman's concern for the wholeness of man requires him to use all the resources available to him for an effective ministry of care and healing. In addition to his own theological insights and religious perspective, the sensitive clergyman will recognize the psychiatric consultant as an important resource for the fulfillment of this ministry. The helpfulness of this type of interdisciplinary cooperation between the clergyman and the psychiatrist may best be illustrated in a parable of Jesus (Mark 4:3–8):

> A sower went out to sow. And as he sowed, some seed fell along the path, and the birds came and devoured it. Other seed fell on rocky ground, where it had not much soil, and immediately it sprang up, since it had no depth of soil; and when the sun rose it was scorched, and since it had no root it withered away. Other seed fell among thorns and the thorns grew up and choked it, and it yielded no grain. And other seeds fell into good soil and brought forth grain, growing up and increasing and yielding thirtyfold and sixtyfold, and a hundredfold.

Man's wholeness depends upon the "seed" of God's love that is planted within him, but for it to grow and bring forth "grain," the soil of man's personality must be receptive. The psychiatrist is a specialist who can help the clergyman analyze the soil of

213

man's emotions. If the soil is too hard from bitter feelings, or is acidic from long-abiding hostility, or lacks the depth of enrichment from arrested development, or is filled with the thorns of ambivalent interpersonal relationships, the psychiatrist can become an instrument to assist the clergyman in his pastoral task of preparing the soil for the nurture and growth of the seed of God's love.

C. N.

BIBLIOGRAPHY

General Readings

1. Clinebell, Howard J., Jr., *Basic Types of Pastoral Counseling.* Abingdon Press, 1966. A major resource for anyone concerned with pastoral counseling. A general survey of the entire field of pastoral counseling in the light of the heritage of the pastoral ministry and the influence of contemporary behavioral science.
2. Draper, Edgar, *Psychiatry and Pastoral Care.* Prentice-Hall, Inc., 1965. The author makes good use of his experience in both psychiatry and the ministry in discussing pastoral diagnosis and care and problems of referral.
3. Godin, Andres, S.J., *The Pastor as Counselor.* Holt, Rinehart and Winston, Inc., 1965. A well-written, practical discussion of contemporary Catholic counseling orientation.
4. Hiltner, Seward, *Pastoral Counseling.* Abingdon Press, 1952.
   Johnson, Paul E., *Psychology of Pastoral Care.* Abingdon Press, 1953.
   Oates, Wayne E., *Protestant Pastoral Counseling.* The Westminster Press, 1962.
   Wise, Carroll A., *Pastoral Counseling: Its Theory and Practice.* Harper & Brothers, 1951.
   Each of these books provides a useful viewpoint for the counselor.

215

Chapter One—INTRODUCTION TO PERSONALITY DEVELOPMENT

1. Aldrich, C. Knight, *An Introduction to Dynamic Psychiatry.* McGraw-Hill Book Company, Inc., 1966. Contains a more extensive treatment of the material of this chapter.
2. Brenner, Charles, *An Elementary Textbook of Psychoanalysis.* Doubleday & Company, Inc., 1957. A concise and readable exposition of basic psychoanalytic theory.
3. Erikson, Erik H., *Childhood and Society,* 2d. ed. W. W. Norton & Company, Inc., 1964. A concept of personality development that emphasizes social as well as psychological factors.
4. Piers, Gerhart, and Singer, Milton, *Shame and Guilt; A Psychoanalytic and a Cultural Study.* Charles C Thomas, Publisher, 1953. Clear definitions by a psychoanalyst and an anthropologist.

Chapter Two—UNRESOLVED GRIEF

1. Bachmann, C. Charles, *Ministering to the Grief Sufferer.* Fortress Press, 1967. Practical suggestions for ministering to the grief-stricken given by an experienced hospital chaplain.
2. Irion, Paul E., *The Funeral and the Mourners.* Abingdon Press, 1954. A Protestant clergyman discusses the funeral as an opportunity for the creative expression of grief.
3. Jackson, Edgar N., *Telling a Child About Death.* Channel Press, Inc., 1965. A guide for anyone faced with the task of helping a child deal with the loss of a loved one.
4. ——— *Understanding Grief.* Abingdon Press, 1957. A good analysis of grief written primarily for ministers.
5. Westberg, Granger E., *Good Grief.* Fortress Press, 1962. A brief description of the grief process written for the bereaved.

Chapter Three—ANXIETY AND DEPRESSION

1. Ackerman, Nathan W., *The Psychodynamics of Family Life.* Basic Books, Inc., Publishers, 1958. Although not written

specifically for ministers, this is an excellent resource for understanding the dynamics and treatment of family interaction and conflict.

2. Becker, Raymond J., *Family Pastoral Care*. Prentice-Hall, Inc., 1965. A brief introduction to family counseling.

3. Morris, J. Kenneth, *Marriage Counseling, A Manual for Ministers*. Prentice-Hall, Inc., 1965. Chapters 6 and 7 are concerned with the type of family constellation described in this chapter.

4. Winter, Gibson, *Love and Conflict: The New Pattern in Family Life*. Doubleday & Company, Inc., 1958. A psychosocial appraisal of marital role conflicts written by a Protestant clergyman.

Chapter Four—SUICIDE RISK

Suicide

1. Farberow, Norman L., and Shneidman, Edwin S., *The Cry for Help*. McGraw-Hill Book Company, Inc., 1961.
   Shneidman, Edwin S., and Farberow, Norman L., *Clues to Suicide*. McGraw-Hill Book Company, Inc., 1957. These volumes, coedited by the directors of the Los Angeles Suicide Prevention Center, can help the minister recognize and evaluate potential suicidal situations.

2. Knight, James A., *A Psychiatrist Looks at Religion and Health*. Abingdon Press, 1964. See Chapter 7, "Suicide: Its Meaning and Prevention." A brief summary by a clergyman-psychiatrist.

Counseling

1. Hiltner, Seward, *The Counselor in Counseling*. Abingdon Press, 1952. A helpful discussion of the feelings, concerns, and goals of the minister in his counseling ministry.

2. Hulme, William E., *How to Start Counseling*. Abingdon Press, 1955. Useful guidelines for the minister with limited training in counseling.

3. Klink, Thomas W., *Depth Perspectives in Pastoral Work*. Prentice-Hall, Inc., 1966. See section on "Dimension and Modes of Pastoral Work" for a description of counseling.

Chapter Five—MARITAL BALANCE

1. Oates, Wayne E., *The Christian Pastor*. The Westminster Press, 1964. See Chapter 1, "The Crisis Ministry of the Pastor."
2. Stewart, Charles W., *The Minister as Marriage Counselor*. Abingdon Press, 1961. See Chapter 10 for a discussion of the nature and goals of family counseling.
3. Wynn, John C., *Pastoral Ministry to Families*. The Westminster Press, 1957. A Protestant approach to pastoral concern for families.

Chapter Six—DELINQUENCY

1. MacIver, Robert M., *Prevention and Control of Delinquency*. Atherton Press, 1966.
2. Miller, Haskell, *Understanding and Preventing Juvenile Delinquency*. Abingdon Press, 1958.
3. Satir, Virginia M., *Conjoint Family Therapy: A Guide to Theory and Technique*. Science and Behavior Books, Inc., 1964.

Chapter Seven—THE WITHDRAWN ADOLESCENT

1. Anderson, Philip A., *Church Meetings That Matter*. United Church Press, 1965. A concise and constructive evaluation of the therapeutic function of group activities in the local church.
2. Dobbelstein, Herman, *Psychiatry for Priests*. P. J. Kenedy & Sons, 1954. Discussion of the relationship of Catholic clergy and psychiatrists.
3. GAP Symposium Number 5, *Psychiatry and Religion: Some Steps Toward Mutual Understanding and Usefulness*, March, 1958. Group for the Advancement of Psychiatry. An examination of the historical relationship of psychiatry and religion.
4. GAP Symposium Number 67, *Psychic Function of Religion*

in *Mental Illness and Health,* January, 1968. Group for the Advancement of Psychiatry. Directed both to psychiatry and to the clergy.

Chapter Eight—ALCOHOLISM

1. Clinebell, Howard J., Jr., *Understanding and Counseling the Alcoholic.* Abingdon Press, 1956. The basic resource for the minister who wishes to understand the problems of counseling the alcoholic. Written by a minister well versed in the behavioral sciences.
2. Earle, Clifford, *How to Help an Alcoholic.* The Westminster Press, 1952. A brief practical guide.
3. Oates, Wayne E., *Alcohol: In and Out of the Church.* Broadman Press, 1966.
4. Shipp, Thomas J., *Helping the Alcoholic and His Family.* Prentice-Hall, Inc., 1963. A clear and concise discussion written by a minister with a unique background of effective pastoral work with alcoholics.

Chapter Nine—THE PSYCHIATRIC CONSULTANT

1. Kemp, Charles F., *The Pastor and Community Resources.* The Bethany Press, 1960. Reference guide to the resources available to community clergy for referral purposes.
2. Klink, Thomas W., *A Clergyman's Guide to Recognizing Serious Mental Illness.* The National Association for Mental Health, Inc. A brief pamphlet outlining the "red flags" that indicate symptoms of emotional illness.
3. Oates, Wayne E., *Where to Go for Help.* The Westminster Press, 1957. Another guide to referral resources, with guidelines for interprofessional cooperation.
4. Southard, Samuel, *The Family and Mental Illness.* The Westminster Press, 1957. A brief practical guide for families who are coping with the crisis of a mentally ill family member.

5. Westberg, Granger E., and Draper, Edgar, *Community Psychiatry and the Clergyman.* Charles C Thomas, Publisher, 1966. A description of two intensive teaching projects for clergymen, with considerable emphasis on interprofessional relationships.

INDEX